Arabic Calligraphy

Ruq'ah Script

Tarek Mahfouz

خطّ الرقعة

Arabic Calligraphy
Ruq'ah Script
Copyright © 2013 by Tarek Mahfouz

Written by: Tarek Mahfouz

Edited by: Robert Johnson and Mark Bitmon.

Cover Design: Tarek Mahfouz , Jose Rodrigues and Moustfa Moqdary.

ISBN: 978-1-304-00547-2

First printing: May 2013

Printed in the United States of America

بسم الله الرحمن الرحيم

INTRODUCTION

أهلاً و سهلاً

Ruq'ah is the newest of the six major Arabic calligraphy scripts. It was created to provide a more rapid and legible way of writing, since the other scripts at that time were difficult to read and write. Therefore, some elements found in other Arabic scripts are missing from ruq'ah, such as:

Vowel signs: Except to clarify meaning or Koran verses

Letter sizes: The large letter size is absent, unlike other scripts: for example, the initial alif is just three dots high

Ornaments: (signs and shapes employed for artistic reasons)

Letter dots: You do not have to write letter dots individually (for example, a dot above the letter could be attached to the body without lifting the pen to write it, two dots will be a dash, three will be a swoosh)

The Hamza of the kaaf: (drawn as a small daal attached to the tail of the kaaf),

Teeth of the letters siin and shiin (just a dash)

Ornamental heads of letters: (not used)

Letter positions: letters may be on top of each other, rather than next to each other, saving space in case you have to use a small piece of paper---ruq'ah actually means "small batch" in English)

Absence of kashidas: Elongation of letters

Absence of divergent angles: Ruq'ah accommodates the natural movement of the hand, which contributes to its speed. Most of the strokes are either circular, curved, or straight.

Absence of letter endings, such as the hairline

The ruq'ah script is used very widely. You will see ruq'ah in news headlines, book titles, street and shop signs, and small verses from the Koran and hadith. There are two versions of ruq'ah; the first being more formal, following certain strict rules about size and shape, and another version, used in everyday writing, that does not adhere to these rules so stringently.

 This book will examine the rules and techniques associated with the formal ruq'ah script. We will be studying pen angles, shapes, spacing, letter formation, letter proportions, line rules, counter, letter groups (ascending, descending, goblet and plate shape, etc.), ligatures, letter similarities, and ductus (the number, direction, and sequence of strokes that make up a letter). I hope that this book serves well as a guide to ruq'ah, which is not only a calligraphy script but also an important part of written communication in the Arabic and Islamic world.

إِنَّا أَعْطَيْنَاكَ الْكَوْثَرَ

The Tools You Need To Have On Hand:

Good calligraphers are proficient at producing their own tools, including pens, ink and cutters. Preservation of these tools is highly valuable and calligraphers are known to not only guard these tools with their lives, but to take great pride in them, for they are the medium by which they communicate God's Word to people.

The Pen:

Start with a bamboo reed about 8 inches long (Iranian bamboo is best for calligraphy pens). Using a cutter (similar to a box-cutter), steady one thumb on the dull side of the blade and firmly press down upon that with your second thumb. Starting close to the ring, about two inches from the end of the reed, holding the reed in your curled fingers, gradually shave away layer after layer. The wood should peel easily. The reed is hollow at both ends, but solid in the middle---whittle gently until you expose the hollow reservoir. Be careful, the reeds can break easily.

The whittling should gently slope downward from the ring, then extend straight toward the end of the reed. This slope is very important, do not cut straight down. As you whittle, brush away any dust left behind, and smooth out any uneven shavings. The reed should get thinner as it approaches the tip end. The back side may be rounded (like a cylinder) or flat.

Customize the size of the reed you will be working with. If you are writing in thoulouth, which uses a 3mm nib, buy a very thin reed. For thicker scripts, buy thicker reeds. Thick bamboo is quite strong and flexible, and is used for fishing rods in the Middle East---in fact, it is often sold on the beach!

The most important step: the very tip of the reed, the nib, must be cut according to the type of calligraphy you will be doing. Different scripts need different angles. This point is thin and sensitive, so do not dig your blade into the wood repeatedly as if slaughtering an animal---use one sharp, strong cut. Use the blade to also thin out the edges of the nib to make your script more clean and efficient. You may whittle both ends of the reed at different sizes, especially to save money.

The most delicate, and important part of the cut is the reservoir, an extremely thin trench cut from the tip a few inches downwards. A notch on the back side, parallel with the first cut, must also be made. The design of the reservoir will decide how ink flows as you are writing.

Reeds of different sizes can be obtained from art supply stores, or online at EBay or Amazon.com at low prices. Another option, in places such as New York City's "Garden District" (W. 28th St. between 6th and 7th Aves.), bamboo sticks can be bought in bulk at very low prices. A bundle of about ten sticks ranging from 3 to 8 feet long costs about 6 dollars. Then you can whittle dozens of pens for yourself, and sell them as you wish! If you feel uncomfortable whittling it yourself, you can have it cut for a few extra dollars.

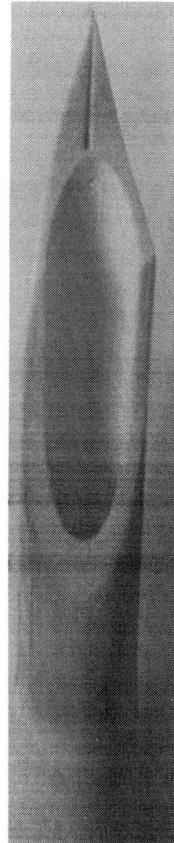

Nowadays, just as many calligraphers use other methods of writing, such as non-traditional reed pens that do not have to be dipped in ink repeatedly. These pens can be found in art supply stores such as Pearl Paint.

Regular ink pens can be converted to calligraphy pens. Depending on the script you want to write with, the tip of the pen should be between 1 and 1.5 mm. First, fill the pen with ink, but do not take the ink jar out of the box, so you do not stain your desk if you spill the jar by mistake. The proper ink must be chosen when using converted pens---many calligraphers use Pelikan 4001 Brilliant Black. Next, use very rough sandpaper to sand down the thin tip, making it wider (necessary for Arabic calligraphy). Use a wire cutter to cut the tip close to a 45-degree angle—not straight across. After this, gently rub the tip against the sandpaper to smooth it—try to do this holding the pen the same as you would when you write, and test the pen every once in a while as you smooth the tip. For a wider nib, you can press harder into the sandpaper, or even use the wire cutters to style the nib to your needs. For finishing touches, switch to an even finer sandpaper, and write letters upon it. The advantage to converting regular pens to calligraphy pens is that they do not have to dipped in ink repeatedly while writing.

These methods aside, any piece of wood can be shaped into a calligraphy pen if one has mastered the technique---even spare pieces.

The Ink:

Calligraphers need to have a large amount of ink on hand, which can get expensive. The cheapest way to make calligraphy ink is to melt gum Arabic and water, which will produce an ink-like substance that can be written with. Besides Indian Ink, which is high quality but somewhat expensive, calligraphers will often use home methods to make their own. The basic elements that go into ink are tea, walnut gravel, water, and gum Arabic.

Although black is the most common ink color, ink can be made in all kinds of colors. Colorful insects were used in earlier times. Today there are many other methods of coloring ink, even food coloring!

القلم والحبر

For serious calligraphers, Arabic numbers are just as important as the Arabic alphabet. To start, calligraphy instruction manuals almost always feature Arabic numbers on the diagrams. Also, the shapes of numbers are often referenced when explaining the shapes of certain letters---the numbers 1, 2, 5, 7 and 8 are referenced the most. Learning Arabic numbers is very easy. The numbers 1 and 9 are almost identical in English and Arabic. The Arabic number 3 is like the English 3, but laying horizontally and with a line extended from the left side. Unlike Arabic words and sentences, Arabic numbers are written left to right, and there are no drastic differences in the writing of the numbers between different Arabic scripts. This book will not be providing instruction on how to write Arabic numbers in calligraphy, but provides a guide to these numbers that will help in your studies.

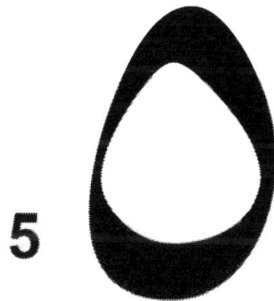

٣ 3   ٢ 2   ١ 1

٦ 6   ٥ 5   ٤ 4

٩ 9   ٨ 8   ٧ 7

واحد	١
اثنان	٢
ثلاثة	٣
أربعة	٤
خمسة	٥
ستة	٦
سبعة	٧
ثمانية	٨
تسعة	٩
عشرة	١٠

تفضلوا

بسم الله الرحمن الرحيم

Arabic alphabet:

This illustration features the letters of the Arabic alphabet. The large letter is the stand-alone form, while the initial, medial and final forms are drawn below. The English transliteration and the Arabic name of the letter are spelled out, and the corresponding number is found in the box at the bottom.

Certain letters will be referred to in Arabic in the book as well as English; for example siin could be referred to as siin; س and also as سين. On the next page, you'll see the Arabic alphabet as written in the Ruq'ah script.

thaa ث الثَّاء ٤	**taa** ت التَّاء ٣	**baa** ب البَاء ٢	**alif** ا الأَلِف ١
daal د الدَّال ٨	**khaa** خ الخَاء ٧	**Haa** ح الحَاء ٦	**jiim** ج الجِيم ٥
siin س السِّين ١٢	**zaay** ز الزَّاي ١١	**raa** ر الرَّاء ١٠	**dhaal** ذ الذَّال ٩
Taa ط الطَّاء ١٦	**Daad** ض الضَّاد ١٥	**Saad** ص الصَّاد ١٤	**shiin** ش الشِّين ١٣
faa ف الفَاء ٢٠	**ghayn** غ الغَين ١٩	**'ayn** ع العَين ١٨	**DHaa** ظ الظَّاء ١٧
miim م الميم ٢٤	**laam** ل اللَّام ٢٣	**kaaf** ك الكَاف ٢٢	**qaaf** ق القَاف ٢١
yaa ي اليَاء ٢٨	**waaw** و الوَاو ٢٧	**haa** ه الهَاء ٢٦	**nuun** ن النُّون ٢٥

٩	٨	٧	٦	٥	٤	٣	٢	١	٠
9	8	7	6	5	4	3	2	1	0

ج	ث	ت	ب	ا
ر	ذ	د	غ	ع
ض	ص	ش	س	ز
ف	غ	ع	ظ	ط
ن	م	ل	ك	ق
ى	لا	ى	و	ه

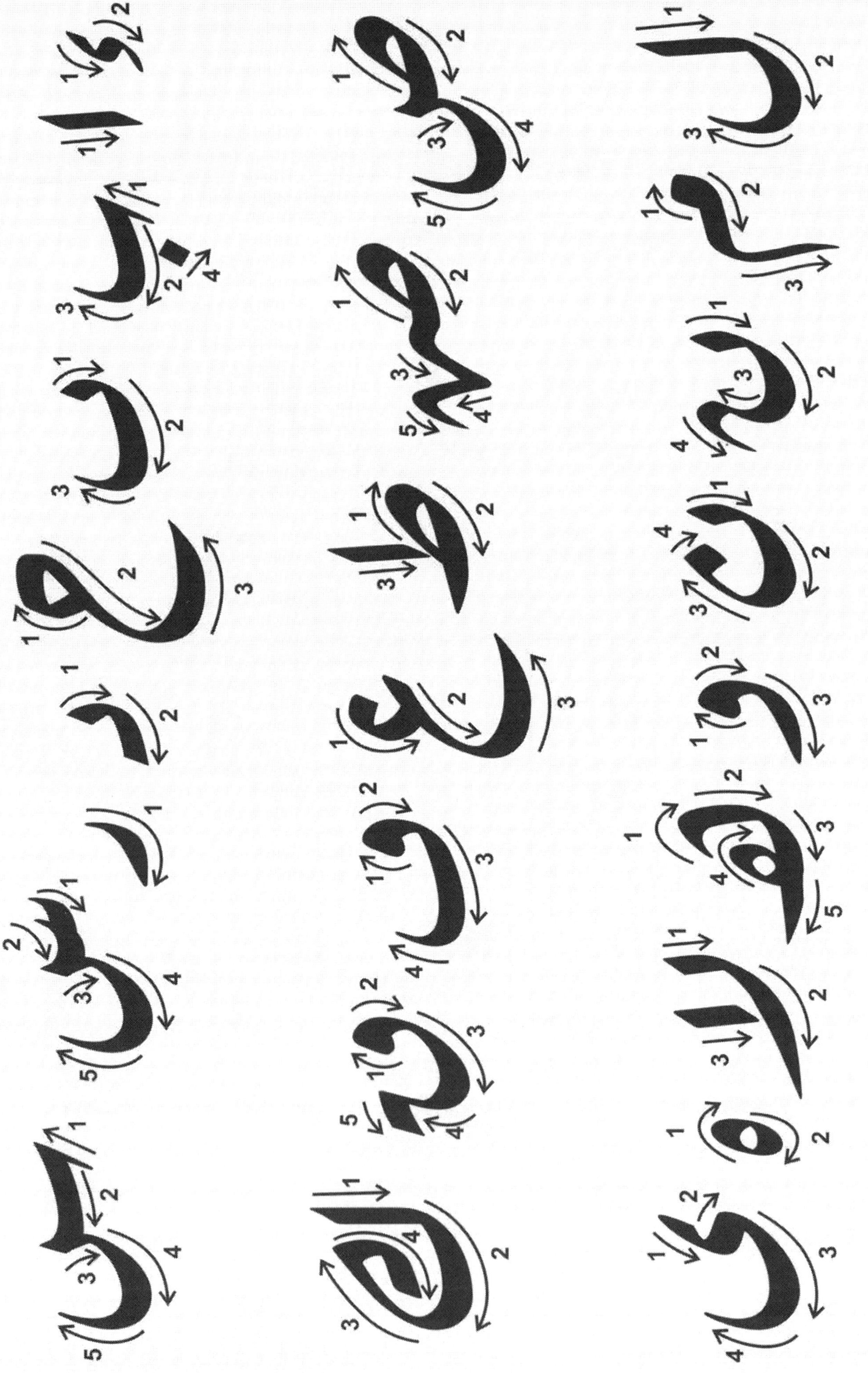

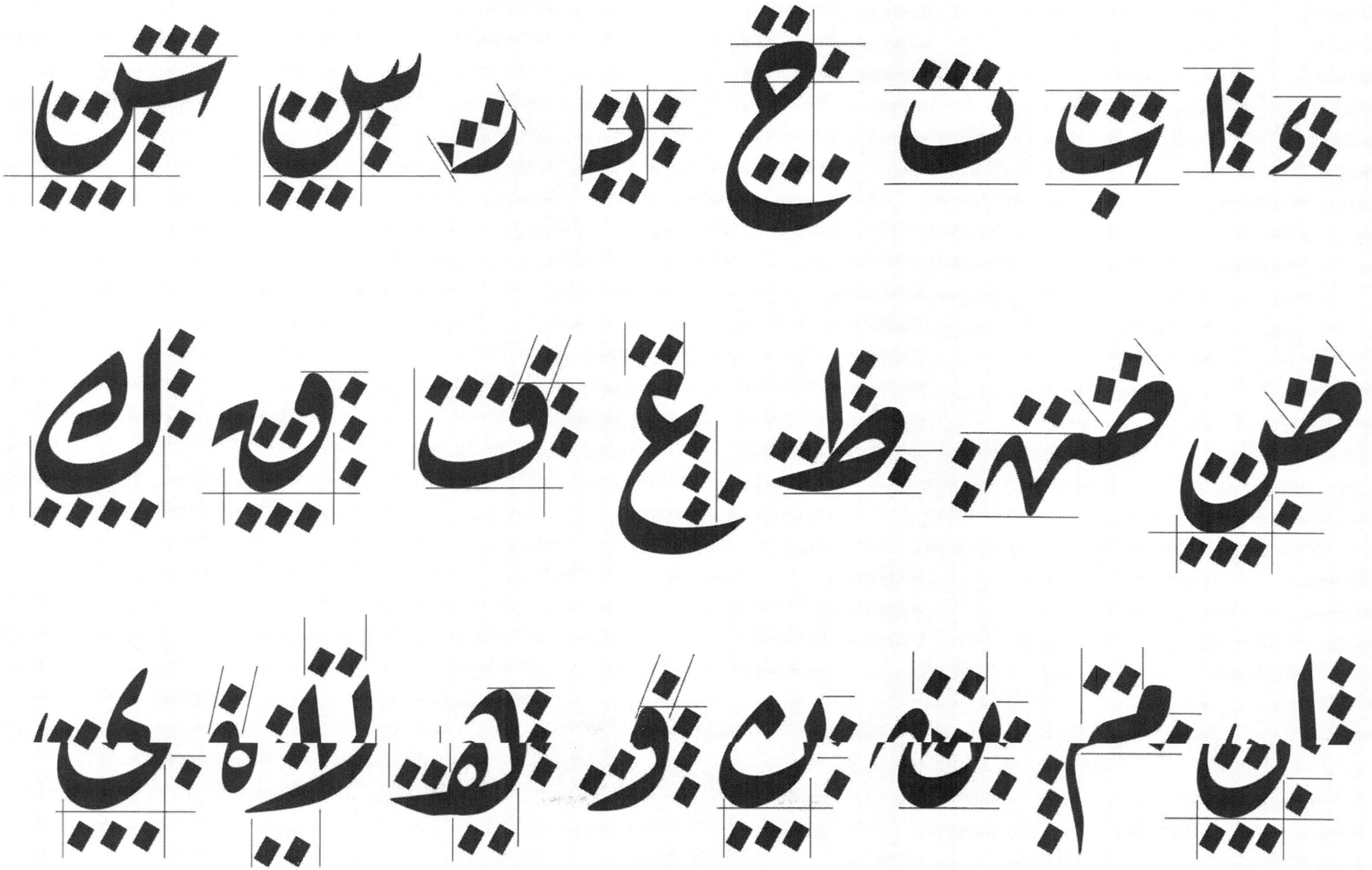

قواعد خط الرقعة

The Rules of Ruq'ah Script:

All letters are anchored to the baseline except jeem, meem, ayn, and occasionally the medial haa, depending on the preceding letters. Beginning calligraphers should use guidelines to assist in maintaining the consistency of this script.

The three guidelines are the bottom line, base line, and top line. The height of the top line above the base line is 6 times the width of the pen you are writing with (pens vary in size). The bottom line is two dots below the base line. These three guidelines are also found in other scripts such as kufi.

Top line

_____

Base line

Bottom line

The letters with rectangular frames around them are the letters that dip below the baseline.

Key Letters:

By mastering several key letters, calligraphers begin to master the entire Arabic alphabet. However, opinions differ on what these main letters actually are. Some calligraphers stress mastery of the 7 letters below (alif, baa, Haa, Saad, miim, haa, and yaa):

ا ب ح ص م هـ ى

However, other calligraphers only stress the importance of the following 4 letters: (alif, baa, ayn, and the "Turkish" noon).

ا ب ع ن

Derivation of Letter Forms:

As this book will demonstrate, the best method for correct letter writing in Arabic calligraphy, is to recall writing a similar letter (or number), either in part or in full. For example, the curved part of the letter noon above is also found in the letters laam, siin, and Daad. Thus, understanding the form of the letter noon is essential to forming various other letters. The derivation of letters from other letters is not only found in Ruq'ah, but in every script of Arabic calligraphy. The size of the corresponding letters will be identical.

Perfect Ratio for Stand-Alone Letters:

النسبة الفاضلة للحروف المفردة

The Perfect Ratio system is a measurement technique that helps beginning calligraphers maintains the dimensional uniformity among letters within Arabic calligraphy script. It is also known as the Proportional Writing system. The width and height of each letter, as well as the smaller parts of the letters, are measured by a system of dots. These dots are rhombus/diamond shaped, and each dot is the size of one pen width—for instance, if you are working with a 1mm pen, your dot will be 1mm.

In the letters below (siin, Saad, qaaf, laam, and nuun) you will see that the curved shape should always be 2 dots wide. Also note that the dots may or may not touch each other. For certain letters (such as alif, which is 3 dots high in Ruq'ah script), the letters do not touch.

Ruq'ah script is especially appreciated for its simplicity and speed. In other scripts, each dot must be drawn; 2 separate dots for the letter taa, 3 separate dots for the letter shiin, etc. However in Ruq'ah, dashes can be used instead of 2 dots (seen in the center figure, and the second figure from the right), and for 3 dots, the figure on the far left resembling the Arabic number 8 may be used.

Half-dots are also used in measuring letters. The triangle figure under the "three-dots" on the far right is one representation of a half-dot. This indicates that the end of a letter is half a dot below the starting point of the letter. A half-dot can also be drawn as a circle. Dots can also be written in numerical form (for example the number 3 is written, instead of 3 dots drawn).

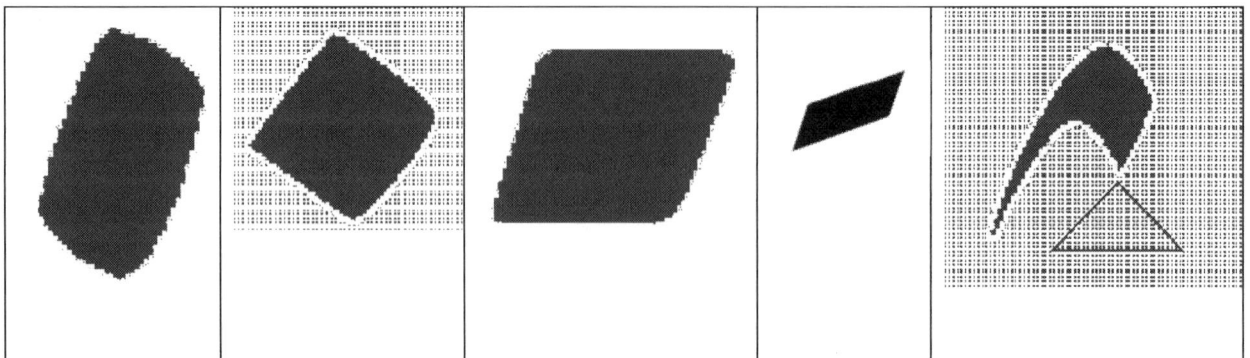

REMEMBER: Only use measuring dots for training purposes. Otherwise, these dots will be confused with letters that actually have dots. Also, colors are sometimes used to distinguish "real" dots in letters from measuring dots. The small lines surrounding the dots, either horizontal or vertical, help clarify the precise area being measured; do not confuse these with the essential guidelines of the script (top line, base line, and bottom line).

Notice that the dots in the figure below are written both ways—separately, or in grouped form.

ش	ش	ت	ت	ق

The letter alif, as seen on the right, should be three dots high. It is slightly slanted from left to right. The diagonal lean of the letter is half a dot in size. The edges are sharply slanted at a downward 45-degree angle, creating parallel lines at the top and bottom edges. The letter alif is usually written above the line but may be partially or wholly above or below the line; this is dependent on aesthetic choices. For instance, in the alif-laam ("the" in Arabic), the alif is sometimes written directly below the laam. As the first letter of the word "Allah", and very similar to the number "1", the alif is widely considered the most important letter in the Arabic alphabet, and many other letters derive their shapes from it.

The Hamza may be drawn on the line, above or below the alif, above the letter waaw, and above the letter yaa. Note that the body of the Hamza is 2 dots high and 1 dot wide.

The letter baa shares characteristics with the letters taa and thaa. Therefore, taa and thaa are not referenced in most instructional books on Arabic calligraphy, except when the baa varies in shape. Baa is 3 dots high and 2 dots wide. Notice that the letter extends 1 full dot above the baseline on the *right* side; however, the left side does not fully extend 1 dot high.	
This is another form of the letter baa. Again, when baa is drawn this way, the taa and the thaa will be drawn in a similar fashion. However, all three letters are 3 dots wide. Start drawing this letter from the lowest point on the right side extension, which should be 1 dot high.	
This is the letter jiim. The head of the letter is 2 dots wide; however, the bottom portion extends 1 dot further to the right. The jiim measures 4 dots above the baseline. The body measures 3 dots high. Careful: the dot at the center of the letter is *part of the letter*, not simply a measuring dot. Notice the head of the jiim looks like an upside-down daal; the head is only written this way when it precedes the letters haa, raa, miim, or yaa. The jiim also has a different shape when it is the first letter in a word. These forms will be discussed later.The same rules and measurements that apply to jiim also apply to the letters Haa and khaa.	
This is the letter daal. Its measurement is quite simple, 1 dot above the baseline and 2 dots wide—as with other letters, measurements vary among calligraphers. For example, this letter could be seen as 2 dots high as well. Do not be confused by the two vertical dots on top of each other—the dot on top measures the height of the letter, the dot on bottom measures how much the letter rises above the baseline. Remember, the horizontal lines between the dots divide which areas are being measured. The daal is written with the full width of the pen, and looks like the first part of the letter baa. This is an important letter for learning Arabic calligraphy, since it is the basis for drawing the first part of the letter haa and the last part of the letter kaaf. For example, the letter kaaf is drawn combining the letters alif, baa, the 3-dot-figure, and the daal. As seen below, to write the letter haa, combine the 3 dots with the daal and the head of a medial faa. (There are only two letters in the Arabic alphabet with 3 dots—the shiin and the thaa). As you may know, daal is one of the six letters that can only be connected to a preceding letter, and not to a following letter. The connected daal looks similar to the letter raa, so be wary of confusing these letters. The same rules apply to the letters daal	

and dhaal.

ك =اب مر ه ه - ذئم

This is the letter raa. It measures 1 dot above the baseline, and the starting point measures 1 dot above the tail on the bottom. The width of raa is 2 dots across. Notice that the raa resembles the base of the laam-alif.	
This is the letter siin. There are three teeth; the space between the first two measures half a dot, the space between the second two is 1 full dot. The curve of the letter rises 1 dot from the baseline, and is 2 dots across.	
In this alternate form of siin, the teeth become one line measuring 3 dots wide. The rest of the dimensions are the same as the preceding form of the letter. This form of siin is used for faster writing. The letters baa and nuun resemble the shapes of this letter.	
This is the letter shiin. REMEMBER: The three dots seen in the image are *measuring dots*. The three dots that are actually part of the letter are attached to the tail of the letter, as a 3-dot shape resembling the number "8" in Arabic, or an upside-down "V". Keep in mind that when connecting this 3-dot shape, the rounded curve of the letter will always become a pointed "V", resembling the number 7 in Arabic, . This "V change" will always occur in letters with attached dots, no matter how many dots are attached. However the size and shape of the "upside-down V" will change depending on how many letters are connected. The shiin rises 1 to 1.5 dots above the baseline.	
This is the letter Daad. It is similar to the second form of siin above, but with 3 dots on the top. The letter rises 1 to 1.5 dots above the baseline.	
This is a second form of the letter Daad, in which the dot is attached to the curved part of the letter. Notice again, how the rounded body becomes a "V" when the dot is attached. The width of this "V"-space should be 1.5 dots. The length of the hanging end of the letter is sometimes shorter than that of the letter shiin, since only one dot is attached.	

This is the letter DHaa. It resembles the first part of the letter Saad, with a column similar to an alif attached on top of it. Some calligraphers adhere directly to this method of drawing DHaa; others alter it slightly. Note the lone dot above the body of the letter, on the right side of the column, *is* part of the letter. The column should be equidistant from both sides of the letter.	
This is the letter ayn. Notice that the head of the letter resembles the number "2" in Arabic. If the letter ayn appears in the middle or the end of a word, its head will be filled in, similar to the letter miim. The head is two dots wide; the top right dot indicates that the head is 1 dot above the body of the letter. The body itself is 3 dots high and, the tail of the letter extends 1 dot from the body of the letter.	
This is the letter faa. It resembles the letter baa with the head of the letter waaw attached to it. Notice that the head of the letter is filled in—the head will be open, creating "counter space", *only* if it is in the middle or at the end of a word. There is a single dot on top, which is part of the letter.	
This is the letter qaaf. The curve of the qaaf is drawn like the curve of the nuun, and the head is similar to that of the waaw—it is filled in only when qaaf appears at the beginning of a word, but it is hollow when it comes in the middle of a word. The head is 1 dot wide, and the first part may rise 1 or 2 dots above the baseline. The two dots of the letter are attached, hanging off the body on the left side, similar to the letters Daad and shiin---along with the nuun, these are the four letters in which the dots can be attached to the body.	
This is the letter kaaf. It may be drawn as the column of an alif, swooping down and up like the letter baa, and curving inwards like the letter daal. Notice that the "alif" part of the letter retains its original measurement, which is 3 dots high.	

This is the letter laam. The vertical part of this letter is also written like the alif, and is 3 parts high. Notice that the letter does not curve below the baseline, unlike in other Arabic scripts. The curved part is similar to that of the letter nuun.	
This is the letter miim. Notice that the head of the letter is filled in. The tail of this letter measures just as high as the alif, 3 dots, however, it extends below the baseline. Some forms of miim will touch or even descend below the bottom line.	
This is the letter nuun. The attached dot in this form curves inward.	
In this second form of nuun, the dot is attached at the end and curves outward. The body of the letter then bends into a "V" shape.	
This is the stand-alone haa. It resembles the number "5" in Arabic. It also resembles the letter daal with a line connecting both ends. When writing it casually in everyday script, this letter appears as a "0" in English.	

This is the letter waaw. The bottom resembles the letter raa, with the head attached on top. The head of waaw resembles the heads of the letters faa and qaaf.	
This is the letter yaa. The first part of the letter resembles the number "2" in Arabic, attached to the last part of the letter "nuun". The head of the letter measures 1 dot above the tail. The beginning of the letter may protrude from the central body of the letter by half a dot.	

The following letters dip below the line:

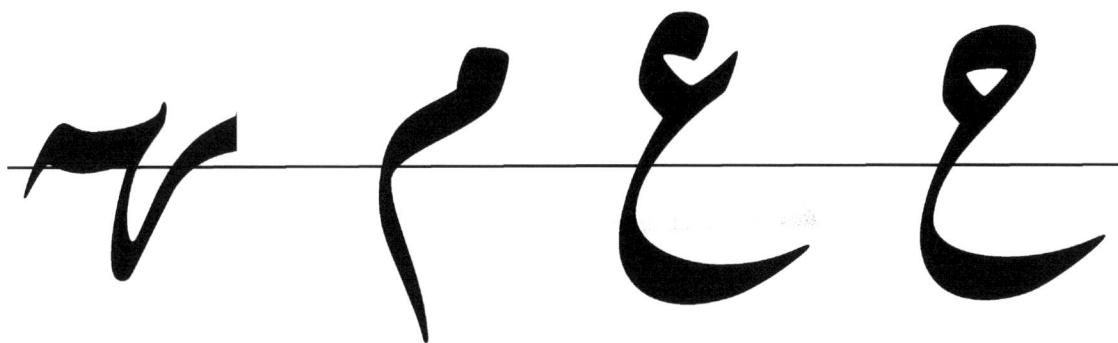

ح م ع م ے مہ

The following letters raise the letters that precede them:

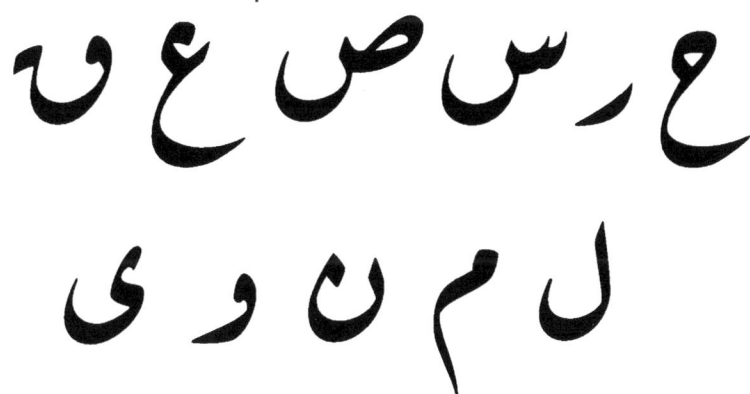

ه ع ص س ر ح

ی و ن م ل

When writing certain words or segments of words, the calligrapher must take these letters into account. If the last letter of a word is one that does not dip below the line, the goal is to end them on the baseline. Therefore, when utilizing letters which raise preceding letters, one must give themselves enough space to accommodate the height of the letters, in order to finish them properly on the baseline. This rule also applies for words/segments that end in letters which dip below the line. All words that have these letters descend quite sharply, as if down a flight of stairs, as seen in the figures below.

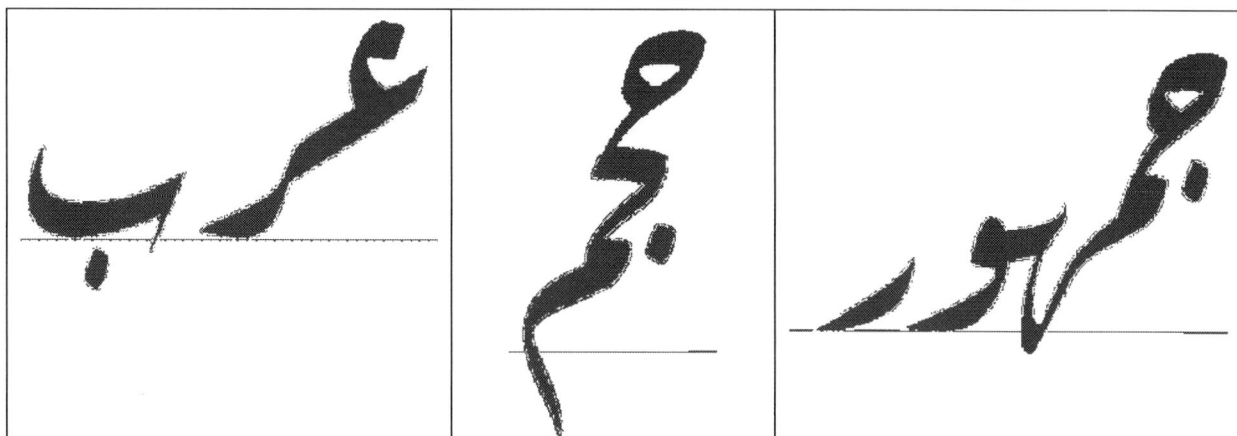

The first word above, on the left, is "Arabs"; the second is "size", the third is the word "crowd." In the word "Arabs", the letter raa raises the letters before it. Therefore, the preceding ayn starts from a high point and descends—the word must not be written on a flat horizontal line. In the word "size", the letter miim raises the letters before it, therefore it raises the letter jiim, and is balanced half above and half below the baseline. Also, the letter jiim raises the preceding letters, in this case the letter Haa. In the final word "crowd", the letter haa does *not* raise the preceding letters, but the letter miim does; therefore the letter jiim is raised. The letter waaw raises preceding letters, therefore the preceding haa only dips slightly below the line, rather than extending far below it.

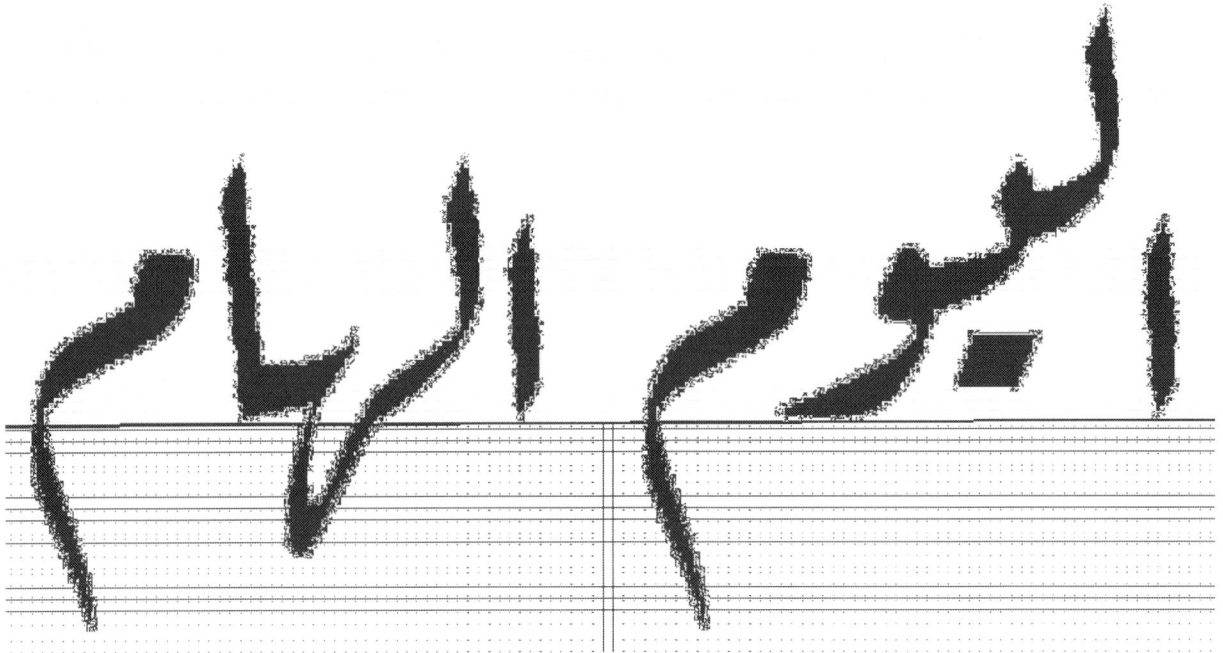

Above appears the phrase "the important", and then to the left of it, "the day". Notice that the haa dips far below the line in "the important", since the letter following it is alif, which does not raise preceding letters. In the phrase "the day", the laam, the yaa, and the waaw all raise the preceding letters— meaning the waaw raises the yaa, and the yaa raises the laam. The laam is not connected to the alif, however, because alif is one of the six letters in the alphabet that does not connect to the following letter. Therefore, the alif is "immune" to being raised by the laam.

Rules for raising preceding letters may be overruled for aesthetic purposes. For instance, although laam raises preceding letters, it is sometimes written on the line, with the alif written under it, if appearing in a word following the definite article "al" (which is alif–laam, meaning "the").

Above is the word "New York" written in Arabic. In the first segment, "New", the last letter of the segment is waaw, or "w." The letter waaw raises preceding letters; therefore it raises the yaa, or the "e" in "New." In turn, the yaa (e) raises the nuun (N) that comes before it. In the second segment, the "Yo" part of "York", the waaw (o) raises the yaa (Y). The second-to-last letter is the raa (r), anchored to the line, as is the kaaf (k).

These letters (laam–alif, waaw, raa, and daal) are always anchored to the line.

Above is the phrase "There is no God but Allah." All vertical lines in this phrase should lean slightly to the left.

محمد رسول الله

Above is the phrase "Mohammed is the Messenger of God." All horizontal lines slant slightly downward.

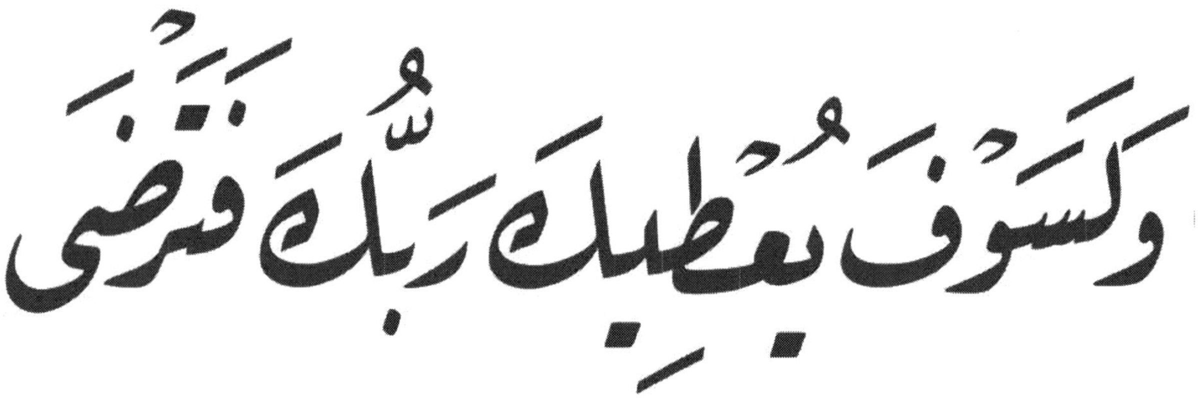

وَلَسَوْفَ يُعْطِيكَ رَبُّكَ فَتَرْضَى

The Ruq'ah style is not amenable to tashkeel, except when writing verses from the Koran, as seen in the phrase above, *"And indeed your Lord will bestow upon you that which shall please you."*

كاهاسا

When horizontal and vertical lines meet, they will always form right angles.

قطار فصام

When the letter alif is connected to the medial Saad or medial Taa, the connection will occur above the line.

عهد

Part of the medial haa will dip below the line, as illustrated above. Note that the last letter is a daal, do not confuse it with a raa.

سمير سبج مبهر

When any letter with a tooth, such as baa, taa, thaa, yaa, siin, and nuun connects to a miim, jiim, raa, or haa, the final tooth becomes an arch as illustrated above.

ب ت ث ج ح خ ع غ د ذ س ش ص ض ط ظ

The groups of letters above share the same shapes.

ع ح	و ف ق	ب ف
س ص ن ل ق		
ص ط ر و د ه		

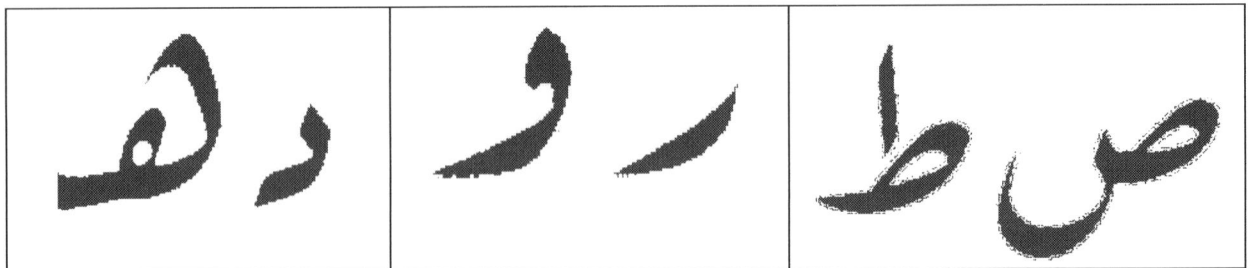

Above are letters which share similar parts.

فففـ قفـ قفـق عـعـع و م

Above are the letters with filled-in heads. From right to left, the letters faa, qaaf, and ayn are repeated three times. As seen, the position of the letter in a word determines whether the heads of letters are filled in or not.

ع صصص طططـ فففـ قفـق هه

Above are the letters with "counter", which have enclosed white space.

المحقق و الدارج

Ruq'ah script has two types. One is the Artistic Ruq'ah script, which is used in calligraphy and must have a certain width and angle, in addition to other specific calligraphic rules. This script is used in writing headlines, book titles and commercial advertisements for its simplicity and clarity.

The second type is the Common Ruq'ah, which is used in written daily communication. It is written using a fine-tipped point, such as a ballpoint pen. It does not have specific rules one must adhere to, but it resembles the artistic Ruq'ah, which people can incorporate to make their handwriting more aesthetically appealing. We can divide the Ruq'ah script's alphabet letters into eight groups.

The first group features vertical lines ‏ا ك ل ط لا‏.

ا ك ل ط لا

The second group, in which the letters resemble a crescent moon, includes ‏ر‏ and ‏و‏.

رو

The third group features letters whose parts resemble a plate. The letter ي is one of the plate-shaped letters when using kashida, although kashida is rarely ever used with Ruq'ah. When not in kashida form, it will be one of the goblet-shaped letters. The plate-shaped letters are:

ب ب ف ك ی

The fourth group is the goblet-shaped letters; their parts resemble a wine goblet. They are:

س س ص ق ن ی

The fifth group features letters whose parts resemble ـد. They are د ه ء.

د ه ء

The sixth group has letters that dip below the baseline. They are ج ع م ه. In the Arabic world, because there are so many rules pertaining to certain letters that share specific characteristics, people make a word out of these letters in order to remember which belong to the group. The order of the letters is not important. People use the Arabic word Friday ة ع م ج in order to remember the letters in this particular group.

ع م عر مر

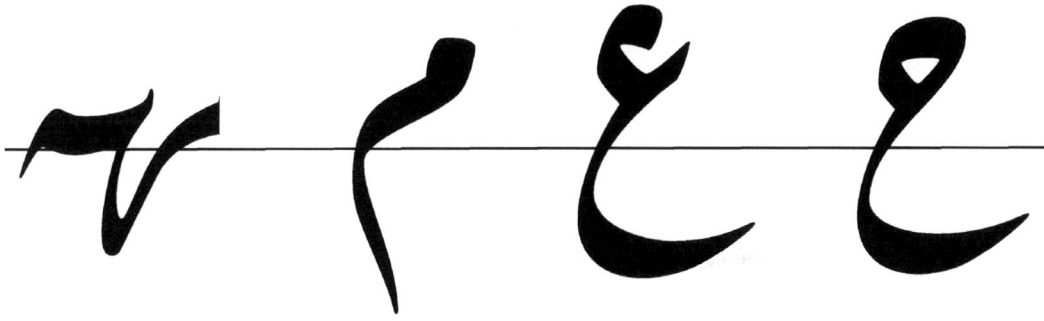

The seventh group contains letters with filled–in or "closed" heads.

ء ف ق و م

The head of the ع is only filled when this letter comes in the middle or at the end of a word.

The head of the ف will be filled only when the letter comes in the beginning of a word or when it is a stand–alone, unconnected letter.

The head of the ق will be filled only when the letter comes at the beginning or end of a word, either connected or stand–alone.

The heads of the letters م and و are always filled in, whether they are stand–alone or connected and irrespective of their position in the word.

The eighth group features words that have a counter or negative space (technical terms for the open space in English letters such as o, d or p). It should be noted that the shape of the counter is different in each letter. The letters are ح ص ط ف ق ه.

ح و ص ا ط ه ه

Dots: These dots help to form the shape of the letter.

م ∎ ، ⬤

Tashkeel تشكيل: Only used when it is necessary to clarify the meaning of the word. These are the Tashkeel figures that could be used with this script.

ـ ل ه ه ﮫ ﮫ ء ء د

Teeth shapes اشكال السنون:

These are the five letters in the Arabic alphabet that have teeth:

ب ت ث ن ى

As long as one of these five letters is followed by an ascending letter, it will have a tooth. You can either include the tooth or not, depending on your writing style. These ascending letters can be remembered by the sentence, بابك به بلابل, meaning "There are nightingales in your door." When written in Arabic, you can see that all of the letters are ascending. All of these words start with the letter Baa to illustrate that when this letter comes before an ascending letter, it can be written either with or without a tooth.

With the tooth written:

بابك به بلابل

Without the tooth:

بابك به بلابل

You must start with the tooth in the beginning of these five letters when the following letters come after it: س ص ط ع ق ق ك و ي.

بسا بصا بطا بعا بف

بق بكا بو بى

32

Do not start any of these five letters with a tooth if one of the following letters comes after i: ن ه د ر.

بر بد به بنا بن

The five letters resemble a swoosh before the following letters: ه م ح.

بحا بم بها

One of the five letters should start with a shape resembling a check mark. It will be followed by one of the five letters that looks like a swoosh (the check mark upside down).

نبه بنج نبی بنم بنها

Sequential teeth:

If three of the five letters that have teeth come in sequence, the second tooth should be higher than the rest of the teeth. If you have more letters, every other tooth should be higher than the last. This is because the teeth of the five letters look like a Seen.

نبت بيت للسلس

General Guidelines for writing الرقعة:

الا سلا طلا ط ل بل ك بك

لب كب با لب بك من هس ه

Vertical Lines:

All vertical lines should lean slightly to the left.

All vertical lines, long and short, should always be perpendicular to each other.

All vertical lines, long and short, form parallelograms that vary in size.

All vertical lines, long and short, should maintain an angle between fifty and fifty-five degrees.

با حاد مر سا صاصاط عاقالب كب مب ن ها

Horizontal Lines:

All horizontal lines are not exactly horizontal as they may appear, but actually tilt slightly downward (both long and short lines), and must be written with the full width of the pen.

ببببل

امريكا اسبانيا افريقيا

المانيا لبنان سوريا

استراليا السودان الصومال

الكويت البحرين العراق

مصر

Isolated / Stand-Alone Letters:

All isolated or stand-alone letters should be anchored to the line with the exception of:

Distance between letters:

The distance between letters is the same.

36

تاج بدر منار

قدر حذر جوع

عال سوس ساقه

طرم هوه نوه رص

طاب عام روح

Alif:

Drawing the Stand-alone alif

Keep your pen tilted between 50 and 55 degrees. Move the pen straight down the page, to make a vertical line the length of three dots. This should look like a parallelogram. Make sure the angle does not change, giving you consistency in the width of the letter. The stand-alone alif does not touch the baseline.

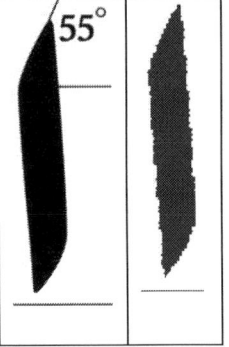

احمد دار

55°

Drawing the Connected alif

The connected letter Alif differs from the standalone Alif, only in length. It is four dots. When you draw vertical lines, the lines are always connected to the letters directly before and after, with a right angle.

طارق

You should always hold your pen at approximately a fifty-five degree angle.

إدارة

The connected الف is longer than the stand-alone الف and connects to the letter before it at a right angle.

ابناء 55

The letter الف is a vertical parallelogram—the opposing sides are equal and parallel. There is a space between the letter الف and the line; this space should have enough room to accommodate one dot.

ار انب

اللبن

All vertical parts of this word look like part of the letter الف and are always parallel to it no matter if they are long or short.

طيران

The circled part of the letter طاء looks just like الف.

بنك

The standing or upright portion of the letter كاف looks exactly like the attached الف.

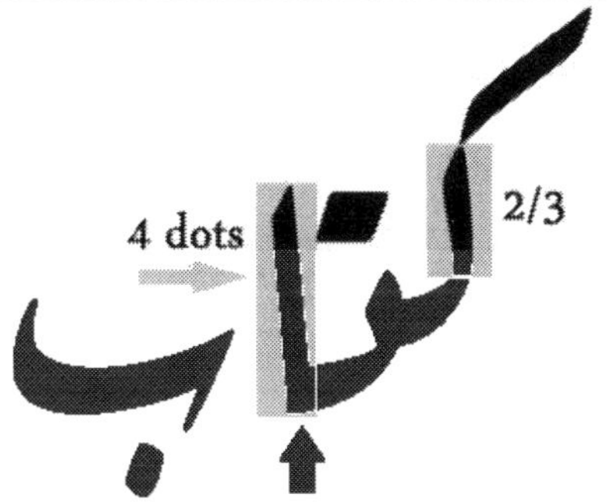

كتاب

4 dots   2/3

Notice the sharp meeting point; it is important to understand this connection is not rounded at all.

البريد

2/3

The vertical lines in gray marked 2/3, above and to the left, are 2/3 the height of the letter alif. The connected الف has a height of four dots.

ايمان

The height of the stand-alone/isolated الف is three dots and is written using the full width of your pen. Every vertical line, even if it is very small, should be at a right angle to the letter before it.

The shape of the alif is seen below repeated in its entirety in other letters:

ال لك بلك ثل لك كك نگك بلك ط لا

The shape of alif is partially repeated in the following letters

ى و س ص ق هل لك

These words illustrate the alif in its different forms, depending on where it is placed in the word.

اسلام إيمان مال جمال

عالم تاج كاتب شاى

قاموس كابوس فلوس عرقسوس

ساعة سماعة ساق سواق

الا يمان يمان

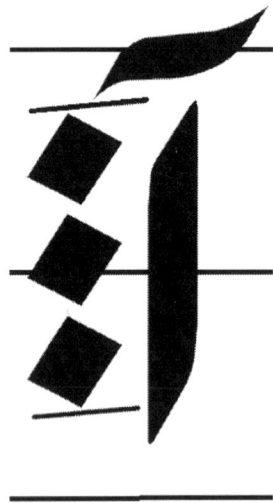

40

اسلام اللجمال از هار

You have to maintain a fifty-five degree angle with your pen throughout the entire writing of the letter.

Notice that the base of the letter lam starts from above the line. There should be a space here.

All vertical lines should be perpendicular to each other.

The base of the لام الف is curved and leans downward; its end is anchored on the line. Note that in the letter لام الف the first part of lam is actually a half الف, while the الف is a full الف. The letter concludes with a sharp point that should be written with the tip of your pen.

الا و لا د

موعظة كرامة مبروك

This medial Alif is the same as the standalone Alif, because it comes after the Raa, one of the six letters that don't connect to the letters that follow it.

Notice that the first part of the Kaaf is similar to the letter Alif.

The connected الف is longer than the stand-alone الف .

This letter is written by starting at the bottom then moving upward. This is necessary because it is connected to a preceding letter.

بيت انتخابات

41

If you were to remove the sign of the كاف the letter would then become لام as written in the middle of a word.

شارة الكاف

The circled part of the letter Kaaf is similar to the letter Alif.

This part of the تاء مربوطة is always vertical; the size is nearly two-thirds the letter الف

1. Both short and long vertical lines should take the form of parallelograms, with two opposing short sides and two opposing longer sides.

2. The letter الف, and all other vertical letters, should be written from top to bottom when connected to letters after it.

3. Any vertical line connected to a letter before it or appearing in the middle of a word should be written from the bottom to the top.

These words illustrate the laam-alif.

ثلاث سلاح بلال

حلال دلال ذلال

علام شلال ظلال

هلال ملاعب كلاب

لا اله الا الله

Drawing the Stand-alone baa

Please note that the bodies and various shapes of baa, taa and thaa are drawn exactly the same way, except for the placement of the dots.

The stand-alone baa has two shapes.

The First Shape: Hold your pen at a 75-degree angle. Make a line the length of a dot. Then continue the line, in a gradual curve to the left until it meets the baseline about 2/3 of the way in. Then curve the line back up. It should look like a boat, with the inside curve the length of three dots.	ب

The Second Shape: From just under the baseline, hold the pen at a 75-degree angle. Draw a thin, diagonal line past the baseline and proceed to draw the boat shape as described above.	ب

س	ثبات	رباب
The initial line should be parallel, or maintain the exact angle, of the line culminating at the end of the letter to the far left.	To begin writing the letter you must hold your pen at a sixty–degree angle using only the tip to form the thin line shown here.	The letter باء touches the line after you have drawn two–thirds of it, just before its movement upwards.
The length of the تاء باء ثاء should be three dots and is written using the full width of your pen.	ت	عنب Notice that the نون letter has a small slanted tooth.

The neck and the curve of the فاء is exactly like that of باء.

تاء at the end of the word.

In preparation for connection to راء this part is drawn with a curve and slight downward angle.

Medial baa has a small tooth slanted to the right.

باء starts with a wide curved stroke.

The letter baa, seen in gray in the figure on the far right is similar to the first part of the letters صاد or ضاد. The باء looks like the three dots of the letters سين and شين in ruq'ah script, seen on the left, and is used only if one of the letters below comes after it.

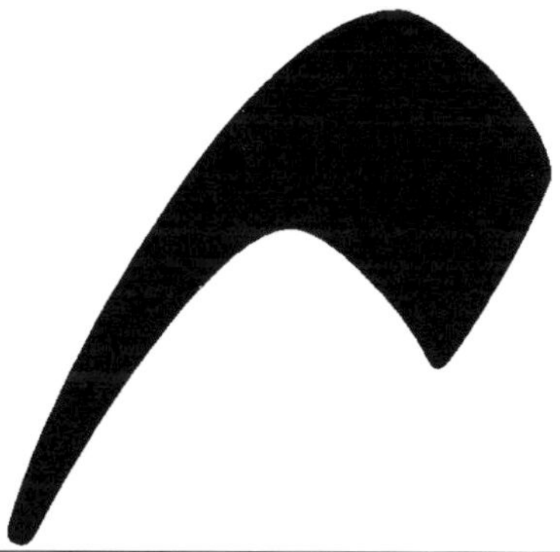

ج ح ح م ه ى

البج الح البخ البها البما البم البى

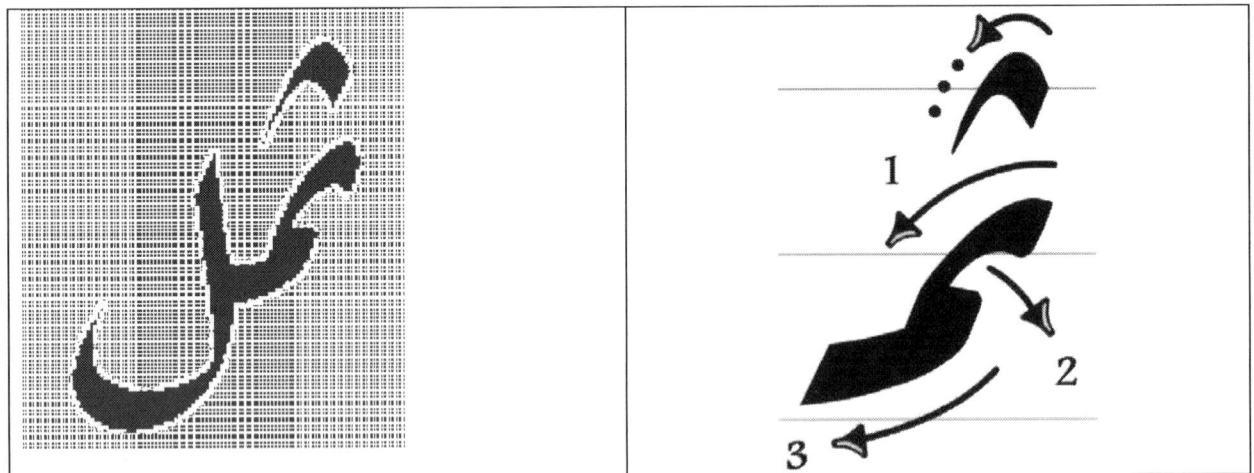

The initial baa may take one of four forms, depending on the following letters. Each of the four forms seen below has small letters above or next to it; these are the following letters that will cause baa to take this

shape.

1–The first form of initial baa is a short, straight dish drawn at a downward angle with the full width of the pen. The letter takes the shape of a parallelogram and leans downward at a fifty-five degree angle; it is written much like الف but with a shorter stroke. This form is used when the initial baa precedes the letters alif, laam, laam-alif, kaaf, daal, and raa (seen below.)

بار بلد بكم ابن براك بدى

2. The second shape is shorter than the first, curving up and ending in a more rounded point than the first.

This shape is used when the initial baa precedes the letters baa, taa, thaa, nuun, and medial yaa (see below)

بير بت بث بن بيض

3. This form resembles the three dots found in the ruq'ah style of shiin and thaa, and it is similar to the first part of the letters ص ض ط ظ. The letter begins at a 55-degree angle and becomes thinner as it is drawn (turn your hand, and not the pen, to achieve this gradual reduction in thickness). This shape is used when the initial baa precedes the letters jiim, Haa, khaa, haa, and miim (see below).

بحر بخر بخار ثمار بهاء بهاء

بط بصل بشير بعيد بغداد

4. The fourth type of initial baa looks like the letter دال. It is drawn with a short stroke leaning slightly to the left that curves at the bottom before connecting to the letters following it. The initial baa takes this form when preceding the letters waaw, siin, shiin, Saad, Daad, Taa, DHaa, ayn, ghayn, faa, and qaaf.

Please note that the rules seen above are occasionally not followed for aesthetic and artistic reasons.

بر تب ثم

These words illustrate the different forms of the letter baa, depending on what letter comes after it.

بلال بیت بشر

بط بخر برهست

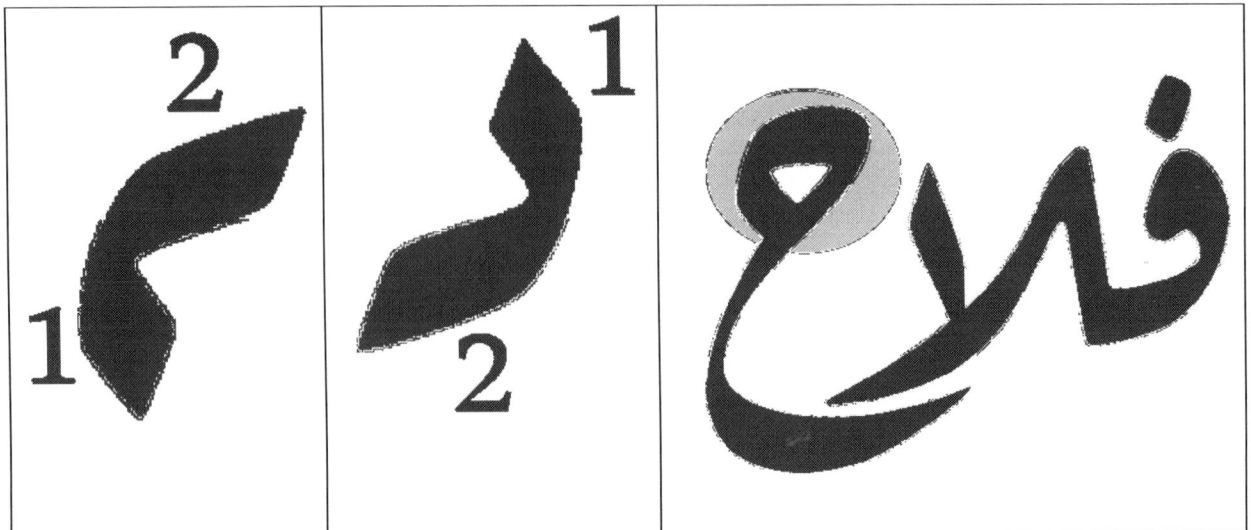

This first part of the ج, ح or خ looks exactly like an upside down ك.

The head of the jiim/haa/khaa (in gray to the right) is rounded in ruq'ah script; there are no sharp angles to this letter as in the other calligraphy scripts. The number 1 in the figure is the end part of the tail, called the shahzyah (shrapnel), so called for its sharp edge. You will see the shahzyah in gray in the letters below (ayn, ghayn, Taa, DHaa).

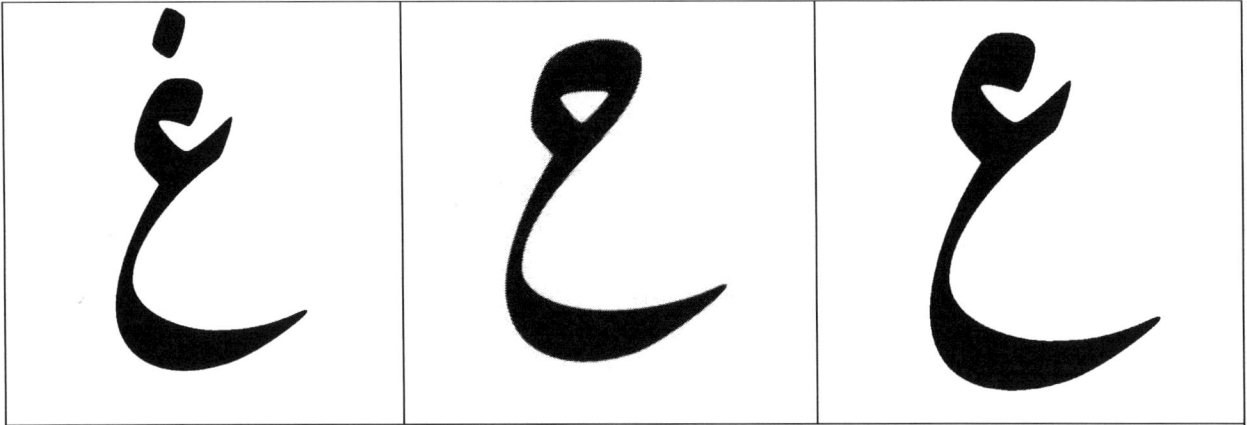

The rounded shape of ج or ح or خ is exactly like the rounded shape of ع.

ج at the beginning of a word has two forms:

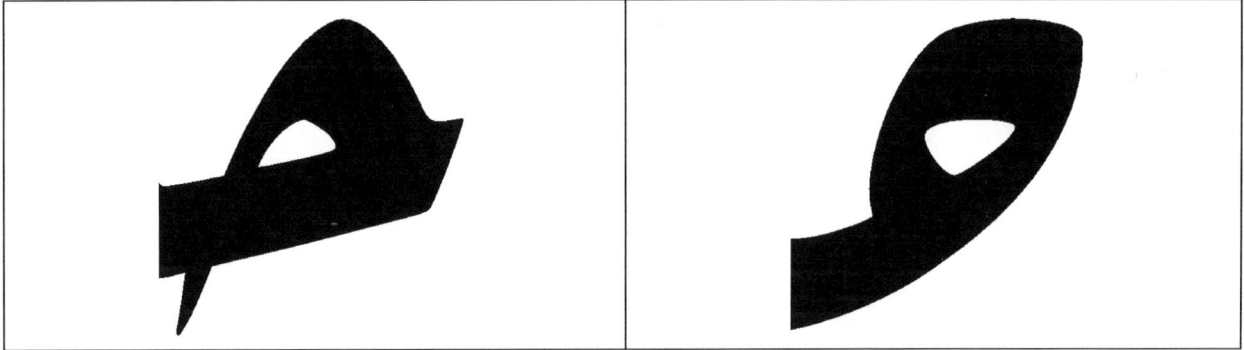

جحاز حرية جهاد جمال ناجي جا

The first form is written like this if one of the letters shown above comes after it

حب خطر حار حلاوة

The second form looks like this if any other letter comes after it.

حول حام حى حيث حيوان

جهر جنة جند جنس جهد

حرم خزف خسر خاص خصلة

لا حياة مع اليأس

حب

ج ، ح or خ at the end of a word

صلح سلح في لى

The parts of the letters ج ، ح or خ seen above in white circles look like the parts of the letter ياء. seen in gray to the left.	Remove the small part that you will find in the isolated جيم.

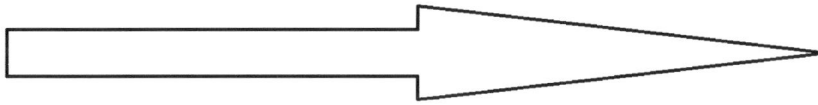

و
و

→

ج ، ح or خ in the middle of a word

مجلة تجارة نحل

الخشب الجلد التجليد لى

53

All horizontal lines are slanted downward and written with the full width of the pen.

احمد بخت قنف نجما محمد

حجر نجم محی جبر کت

نجر مجر سکو فجر عجب

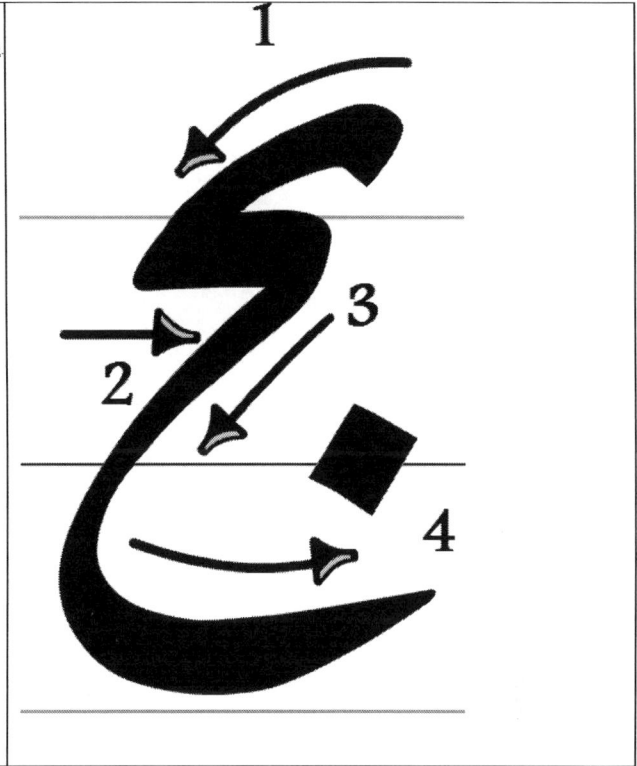

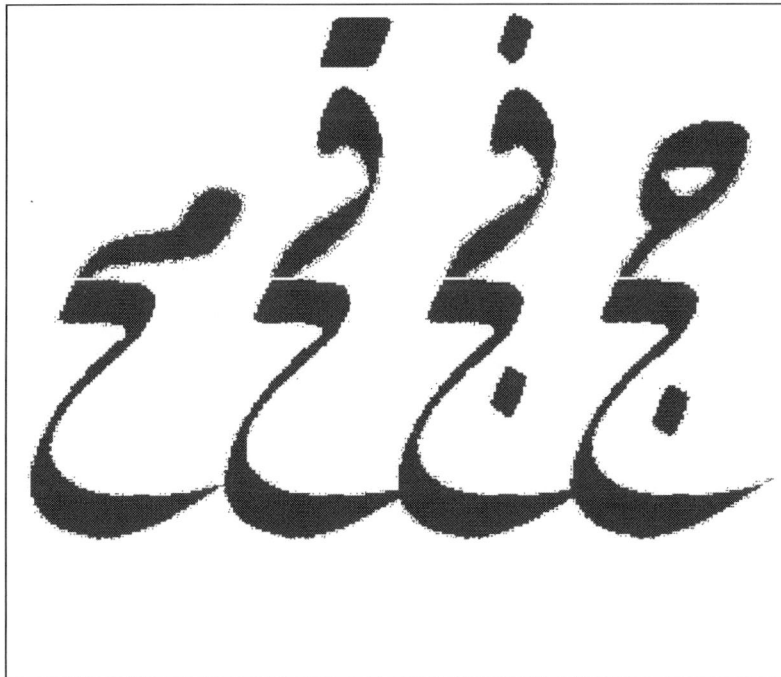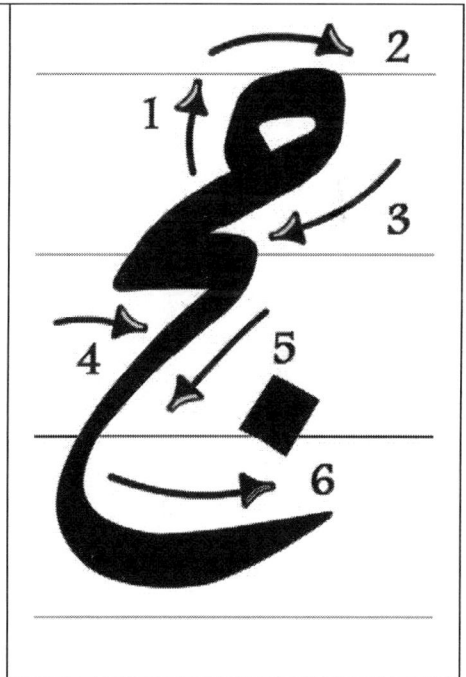

55

Daal:

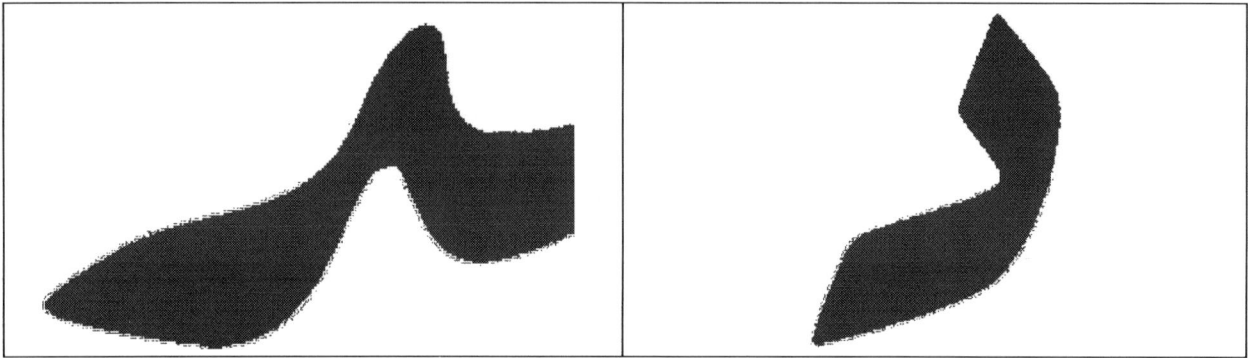

Drawing the Stand-alone daal

Hold the pen between 55 and 60 degrees, then draw a small, diagonal dash to the right, the length of one dot. Then curve down to the left and touch the baseline at the tip.

The horizontal, or second section, is not perfectly horizontal but is written with a slight downward angle like all other horizontal lines.	The first part is upright though not exactly vertical as it leans a bit to the right.	الدال is drawn with two strokes; the second is longer than the first.
	The top part, like the الف, is fifty-five degrees.	The two parts meet to form a nearly perfect right angle.

The first part of الجيم, الحاء or الخاء is merely an upside down دال.

The rules that apply to الدال also apply to الذال.

درس دس	سب	سے مدرس	درس
دفع	دهدر	دعی	سعد
دل	سد	حد	مهد

57

Raa

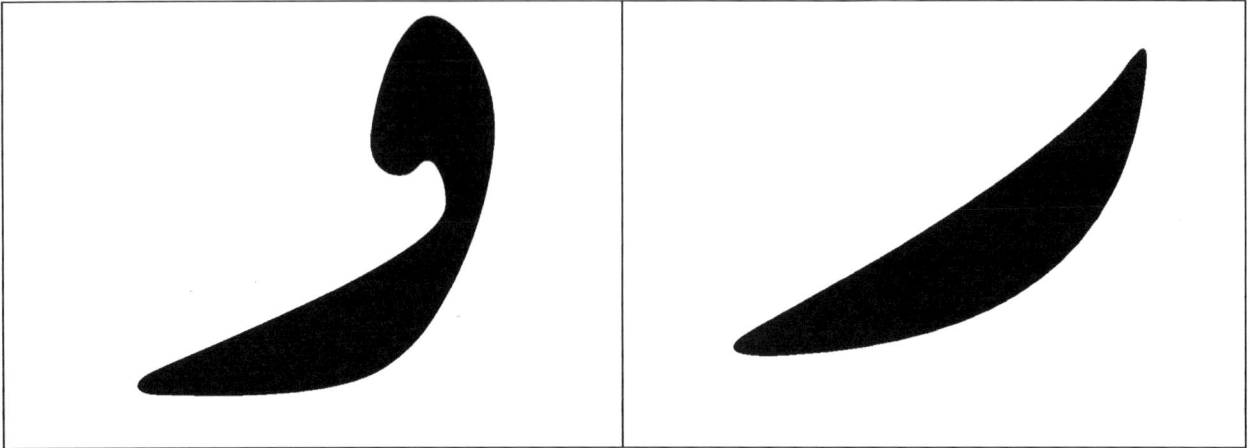

الراء and الزاي is written exactly like الواو.

The way to write it is as follows:

Begin by drawing a long straight line at a downward angle to the left, this line is written with the tip of your pen.

Next, again with the tip of your pen, draw a curved bottom line that reattaches or meets the initial line upon completion. The body of the واو is also written this way.

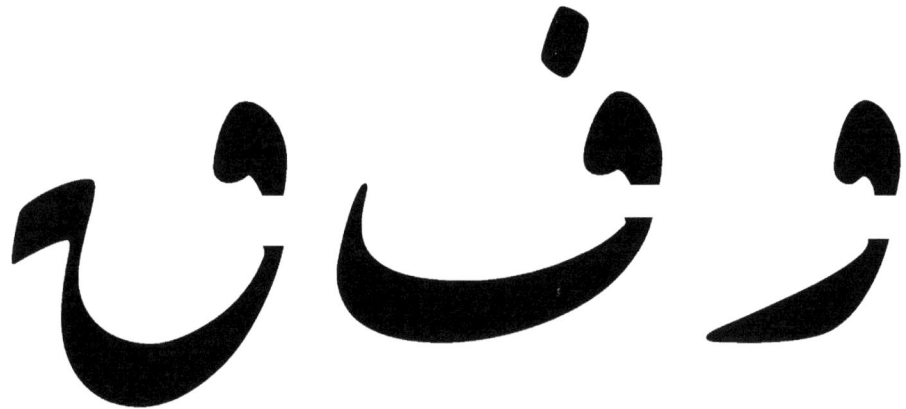

The head of the واو is exactly like the head of either the الفاء or the القاف.

The same rules for writing الراء also apply to الزاي.

This letter is called الزاي and not الزاء.

عبور   مرور   ورود   ارز

مرور	مزدور	دور
نور	عور	فور
فور	طور	صور

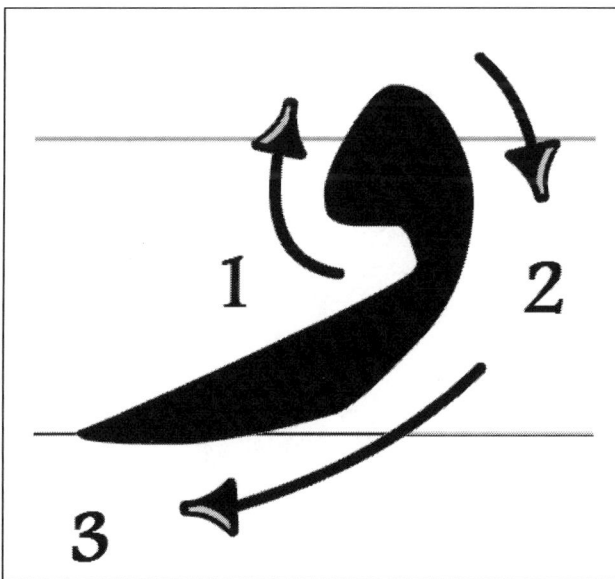

To draw the connected daal, move your pen slightly upward to the left, curving at the top before bringing the pen sharply down to the left at a steep angle. This should not be drawn like a connected alif.

When drawing the الراء you must imagine a line drawn through what may be considered the center of the letter. The line is drawn at an angle. The outer edge at the bottom of the الراء and the inner edge just above it maintain the exact same angle.

This same method holds true for the longest edge of the triangular bottom of the letter where that side and the underside, or exterior of the central to top portion of the letter also maintain the exact same angle.

This section of daal is not sharp but rounded.	This part has a triangular shape where the longest side is the top. This longest side is not perfectly horizontal but instead leans at a slight downward angle to the left.	Move your pen slightly upward, curving at the top, before bringing the pen sharply down to the left at a steep angle, this should not be written like the connected الف.	This part connected to دال is written with the full width of the pen and leans downward like the rest of the horizontal lines.

	The connected راء also looks like a triangle and is similar in appearance to دال. They are both written with the tip of the pen; the empty interior of the letter is filled in with the tip of the pen. These two parts are connected directly without the standard thin line.	This part connected to the راء leans downward as is standard for all horizontal strokes.

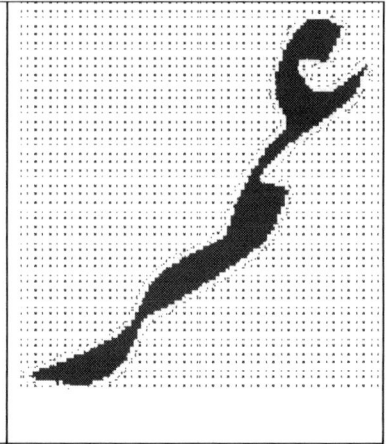		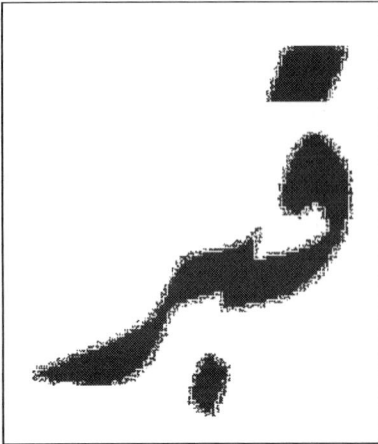
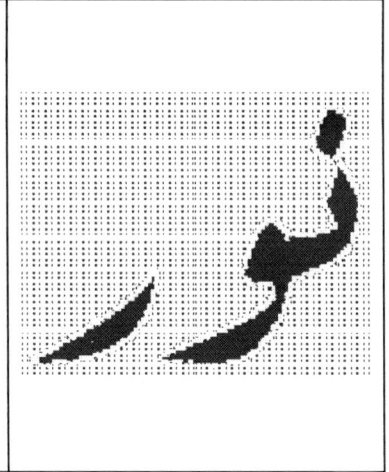	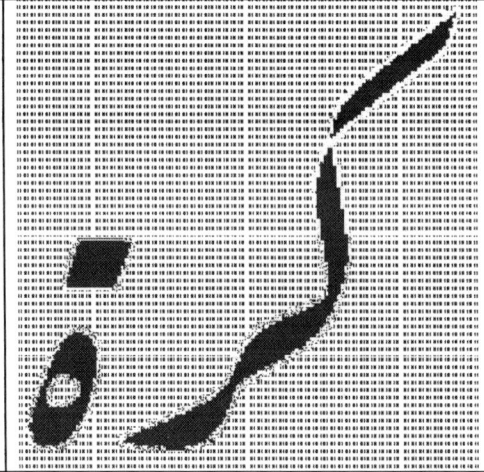	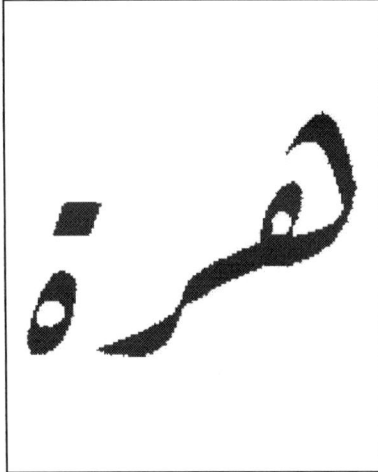
		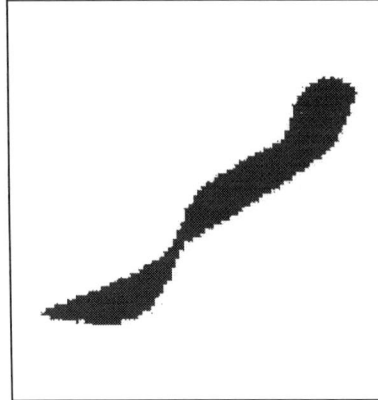

سين and شين are both very easy to write، you simply draw a slanted dash written with the full width of the pen. Just like all other horizontal letters, they are written at a downward angle.

The dash of سين and شين always makes a right angle when connected with any vertical line. The dash is slanted downward.

90°

To draw this slanted area hold your pen at a fifty-five degree angle and move upward.

This part of the letter points back to the right.

The tooth should be slightly rounded.

This area curves in preparation to be connected to ميم.

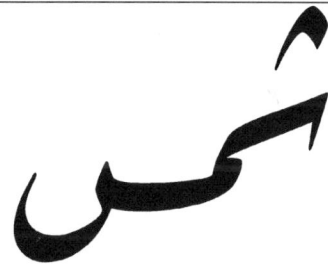

This curved area of the letters سين and شين is exactly like the curved areas of ن, ض, ص and ل

This is a wide tooth like the tooth found in شيء.

The الشين (above right) is different than the سين (above left) only at the very end of the letter. Notice the that curve at the end of الشين is in fact the three dots.

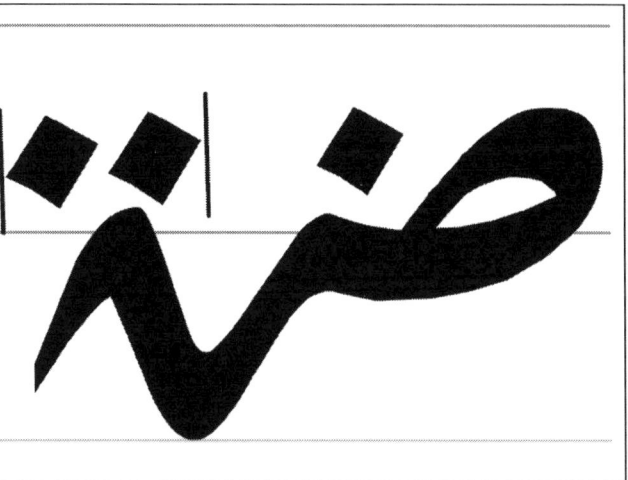

سه

Contrary to what many people believe, you can write سين in the Ruq'ah style with three teeth.

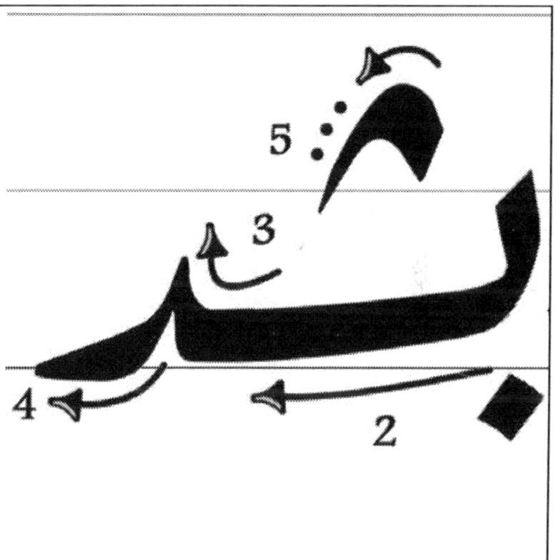

ساعة سلك سكر سلام

سماء مسجد الشمس الناس

Each of the two areas pointed out with arrows are drawn with sharp angles.

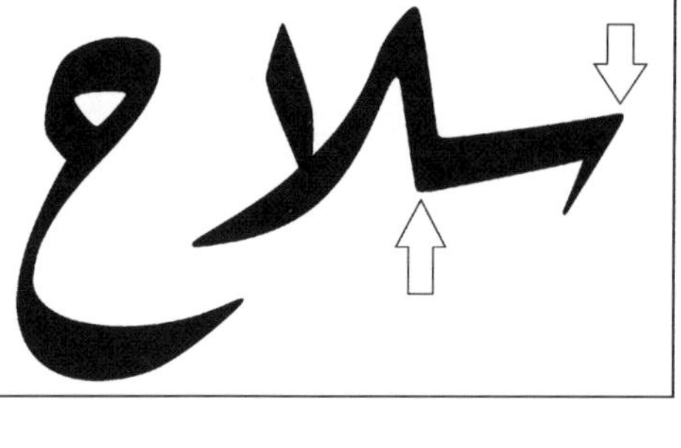

Drawing the Stand-alone Saad

To draw the Saad, hold your pen at a 65-degree angle. Draw a short, thin line upwards, then curve around and down to the right, looping around to touch and pass the starting point. This loop ends in an upward line, then the next line dips deep to the left to form the goblet. The short, thin beginning of the letter is actually the three dots of the shiin or thaa, while the curved underside is formed by a part of the letter baa. The goblet is the same as that of the letter nuun.

The rising curved area is longer than the looping section at the extreme right hand side of the letter.

Maintain an angle of fifty–five degrees while drawing this rising portion of the letter.

This is not a sharp angle, it should be written with a curve.

Unlike the حاء, there is no downward tooth.

The first tooth of صاد leans to the right, just as the tooth found in سين.

The start of the letter is lower than the end of the loop.

The second part of the letter صاد is curved downward.

الصلاة

Unlike other styles this area is always rounded even where it meets the following letter, it does not meet at a sharp angle and therefore does not have a sharp tooth.

الصبر الصيدلية

المقص

The first curved section looks like the first part of دـ.

د

الرصاص

The curved part of الصاد is as the curved parts found in س, ل or ن.

صانف صورب صهر صمم

نصب عصب مصد نصر

ناقص عرض قبض ركض

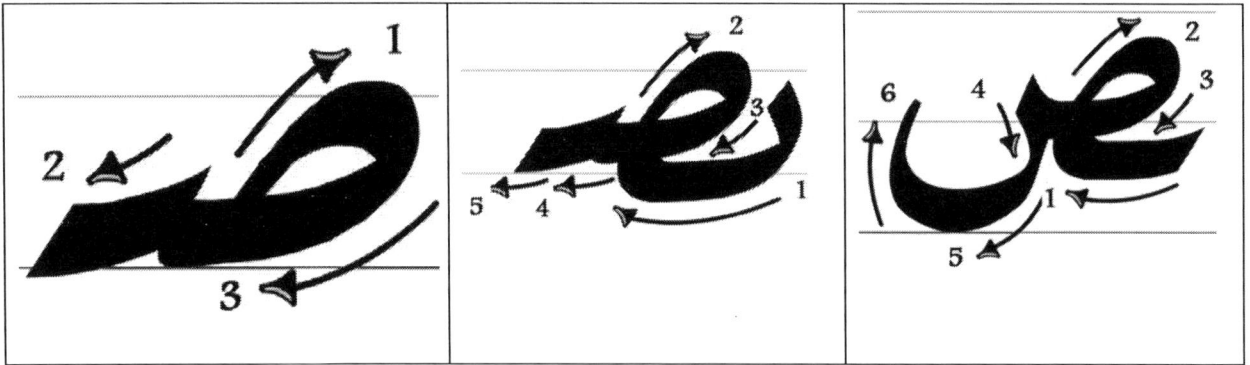

Drawing the Stand-alone Taa

The Taa is drawn similarly to the Saad, however, hold your pen at a 50-degree angle (however, this rule is not always followed). Draw a short, thin line upwards, then curve around and down to the right, looping around to touch and pass the starting point. The head resembles that of the Saad, but is slightly more elongated. There is no goblet to the left of this, however there is a vertical column (alif) floating above the taa.

If there are three consecutive teeth, the middle tooth is higher.

Notice the curvature of the letter طاء in preparation to be connected to the letter هاء.

Remember that the connected راء is written like a small triangle but with rounded edges. The transition between these two letters is rounded and not jagged or sharp.

The letter طاء ends with a sharp point.

Just before finishing the letter trace the outer edge with the tip of your pen and then go back afterward to fill it in.

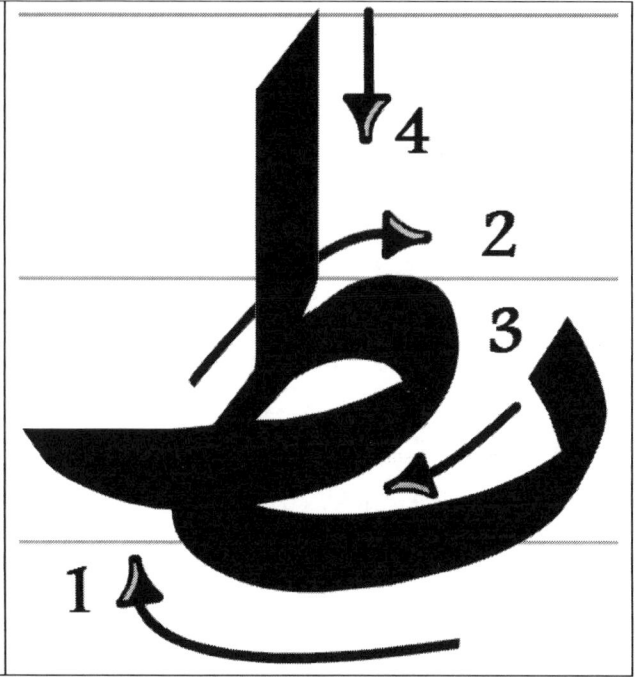

شارع علم عدل عماد عيادة

Drawing the Stand-alone ayn

Hold your pen at approximately 60 degrees. Draw a small "c" with the tail cut off, or a number 2 in Arabic. Then pick up your pen and place it slightly to the right of the middle of your first stroke. Your second stroke is similar to the shape of the jiim, so curve down to the left, dip below the baseline and curve up, and taper out.

The start of the letter عين whether it is isolated or at the beginning of a word looks like the Arabic number two in Ruq'ah script.	عً ٢

This rounded shape of the letter عين is similar to the rounded portion of ج, ح or خ.

Note the way that this bottom portion protrudes out beyond the top part of the letter.	عً

The downward slanted horizontal dash is written with the full width of the pen held at a fifty-five degree angle as if you were writing the beginning of الف.

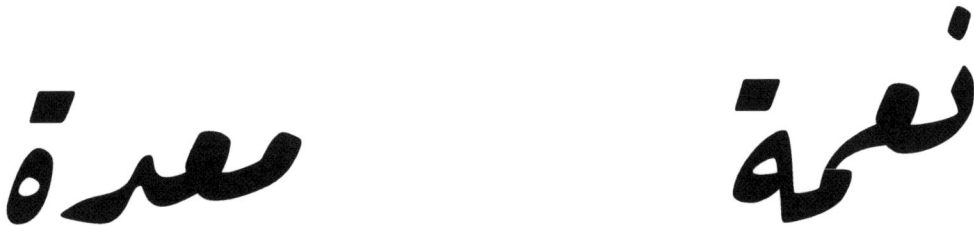

نعمة   معدة

The letters shown above illustrate the way العين or الغين are written in the middle of a word.

1–The head of the final عين looks like the medial form of عين. 2–This rounded end of the letter ayn resembles the rounded end of the letters jiim/haa/khaa. خ ح ج	

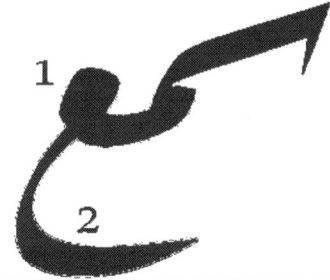

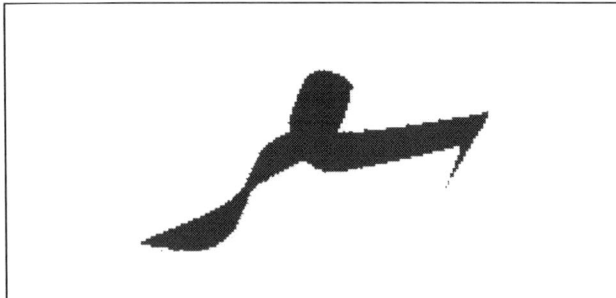

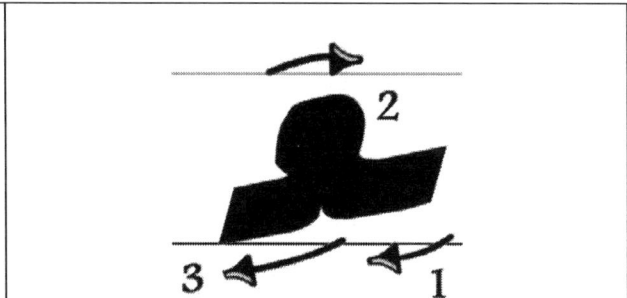

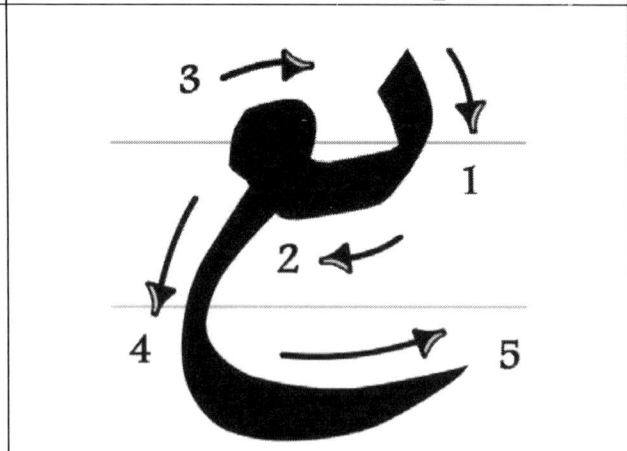

Drawing the Stand-alone faa

Hold your pen at a 60-degree angle, then spiral around and curve out to the left as if you are drawing a baa. Then draw a dot above the spiral, and this will produce the letter faa.

فداء	عفاف This area should always maintain a downward angle like all horizontal lines.	فرد This is a slanted dash that curves at the end in preparation to connect with the letter راء.
مقاول The head of the قاف or فاء should always be leaning to the right. When transitioning from the letter قاف to الف make sure to leave a slight angle before committing to the straight line.	قمر	ريف
برقوق The dots of القاف lean downward.	الطريق قاف is filled in when it occurs in the middle of a word.	When الفاء or القاف are found in the middle of a word, they look like هاء. القاهرة

73

قمل | قبقاب قميص | The neck of قاف is longer.

The head of فاء or قاف should be filled in if used at the beginning of a word.

The head of فاء or قاف in the middle of a word should left open and not filled in.

Only the head of فاء will be open at the end of a word, the head of القاف should be open if it comes at the end of a word.

فففف

ققق

هـ ق	ف	و

The head of the الواو is the same as the heads found in both الفاء and القاف with the exception of the neck of the letter قاف , which is longer.

Writing the Head:	
Start by holding your pen at a fifty–five degree angle and write a figure that looks like an Arabic comma (،) but instead of just completing the comma roll the pen to make a right curve, filling in the head. In the case of the head of the letter قاف the neck should be long.	ٯ

The body of واو is exactly like the body of الراء and is drawn with the tip of your pen.	ر	و

The rounded area of the letter فاء looks exactly like the rounded area of the letter باء.	ب	ف

4-The two dots of قاف are attached to its body and point or lean downward. 5-This is the thickest part of the letter.	3-Maintain the curve as you move your pen upward.	1-A steep curve. 2-The second curve is rounded and there are no sharp edges.

فوق فاق قفى فوض فو نفق

نفق فلق قبو قذف قرف وقر

وقر وفد عقب قاب فقر وفق

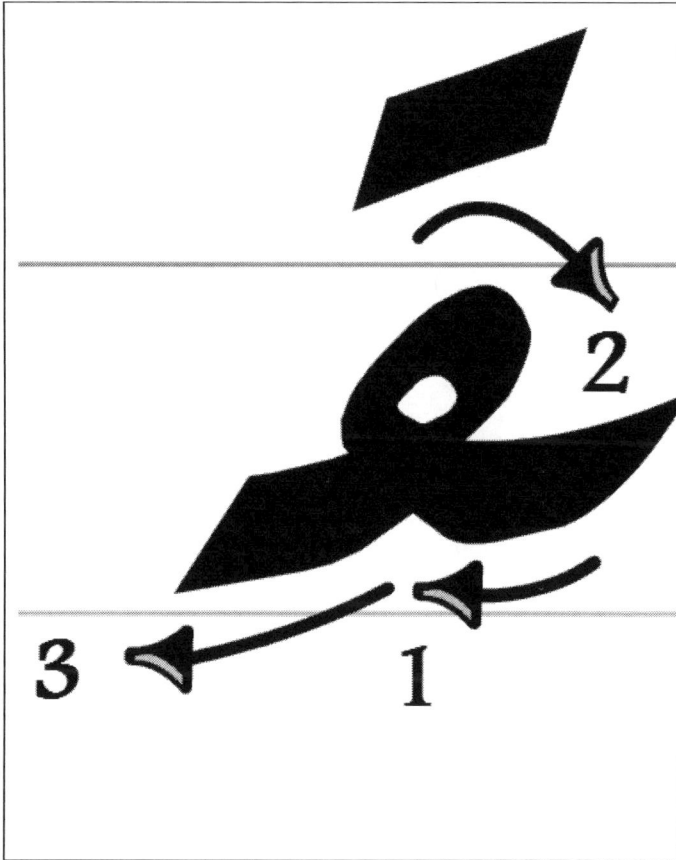

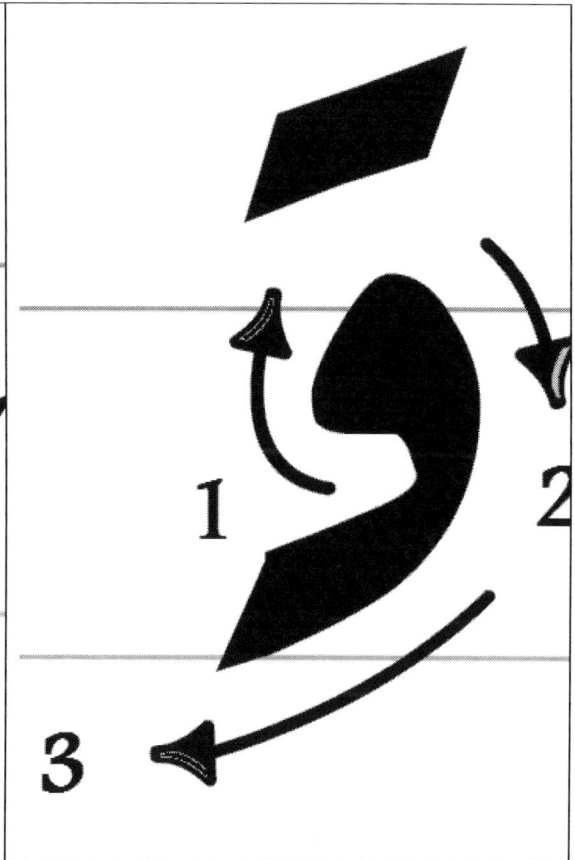

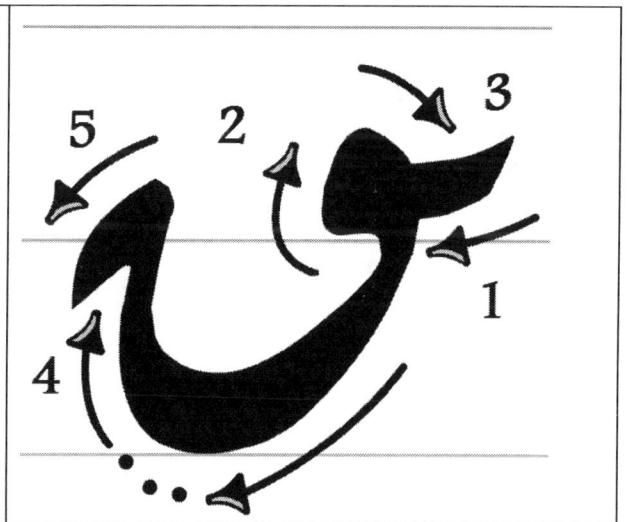

When you write this letter, it is important to know that the interior spaces are constant and proportionate to each other.	The inside part at the end of the letter كاف is similar to that found in دال. The separation between the figure that looks like الف and the body of كاف rises slightly above the line.	(1) This is where you start writing the letter كاف, if you have a line under it, it will touch the line but not go below it. The bottom portion of the letter is curved, it then moves upward to form a loop that finishes by circling back around to point at the first curved section.	This looks exactly like الف. This area of the letter is thin and created by turning your hand. This rounded shape looks like the rounded shape of the letter باء.

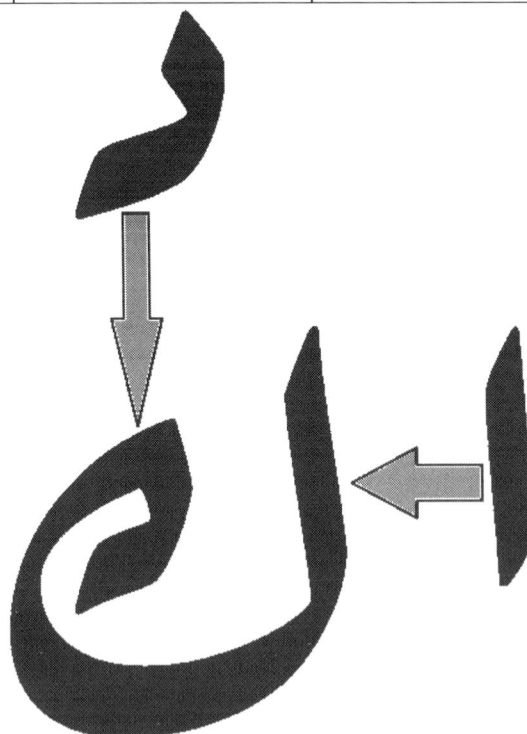

كاف **at the beginning of a word has two shapes**

The sign of the كاف looks like a steep leaning parallelogram. 	Then draw the letter دال. Maintain a space between the sign of the كاف and the sign that looks like الف. 	The first version of the shape: Draw the part that looks like the three dots. 

This type of كاف connects only with the letters shown above. کل

The second version of the shape:

Similar to the letter لام at the beginning of a word, the only difference is that you must add the sign of the كاف.

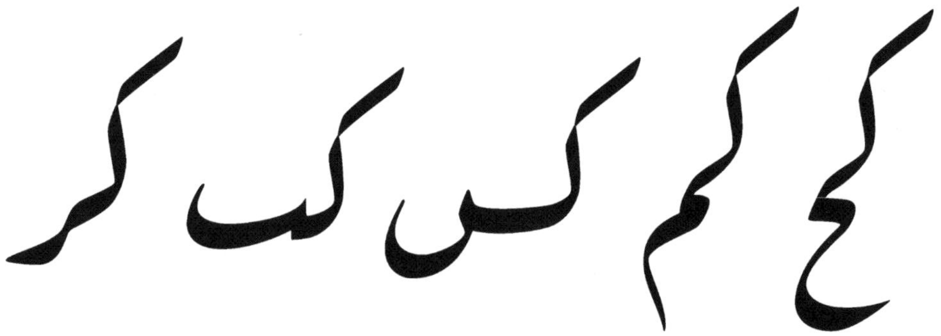

The letter لام touches the line without dipping below it, and then moves upward again.	The inner space has a width of two dots. The end of the letter is curved to the right.	The stand–alone لام consists of the stand–alone الف with the addition of the rounded part from ي ن ص س.

لام at the beginning of a word: This is the shape of lam if followed by these letters: م ج ح خ ي

And this is the shape if followed by these letters: ص ض ط ظ.

لوف	لبس	لندن	لعب

ب

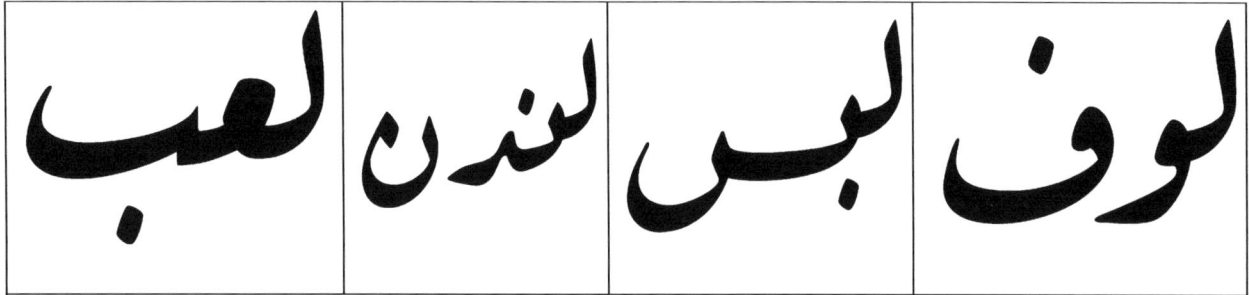

This shape is used for all other letters.

لام at the end of a word; exactly like the stand-alone لام.

سبيل

When more than one letter precedes the لام the connection happens below the middle of the "alif" part of laam.

خل

When only one letter precedes the لام, it connects to the middle of the "alif" part of لام.

لبن ليمون لحم المياه عدلى

اللام always looks like الف, but the shape of the connection to the following letter varies. It will have a different form depending on which letter comes after it.

ج خ ح لم لى

The following letters ج ح خ م ي are always written under the lam.

The end of the letter ميم should be thin and written with the side of the pen.

قلم بلح جليد قلب عملية

المال منديل سبيل الحبل

1. Remember that the beginning of the letter عين looks like the Arabic number two.

2. All horizontal lines always lean downward whether the line is long or short.

3. Remember that all vertical lines are parallel to each other.

4. The connection to the letter lam occurs in the middle only if it is connected to one letter. It will occur under the middle if it is connected to more than one letter.

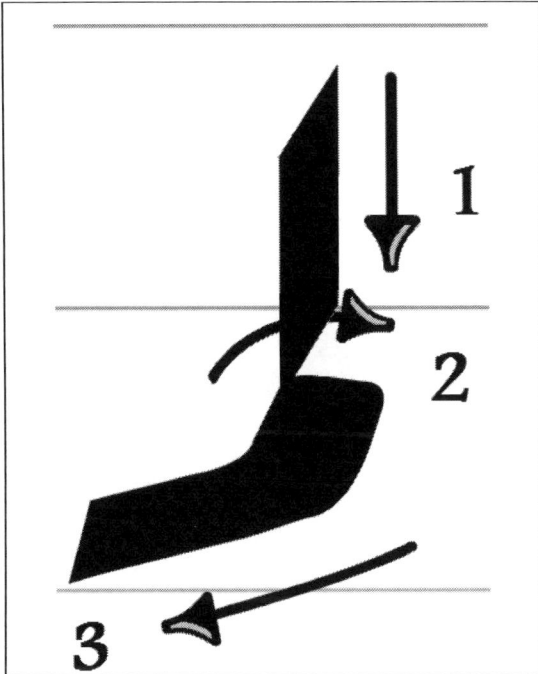

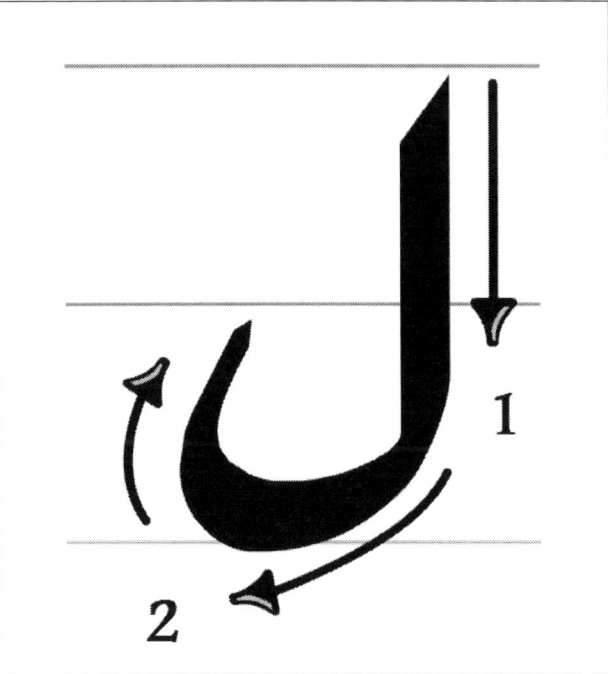

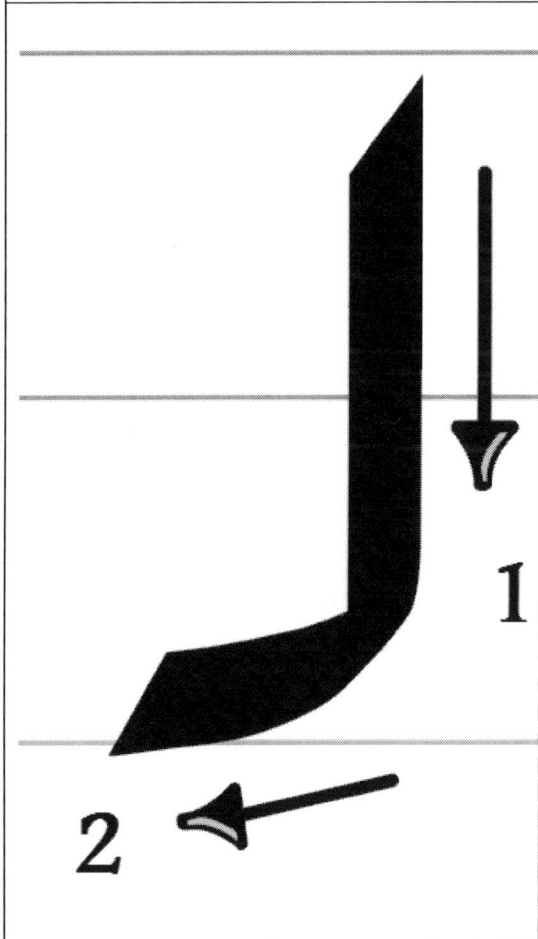

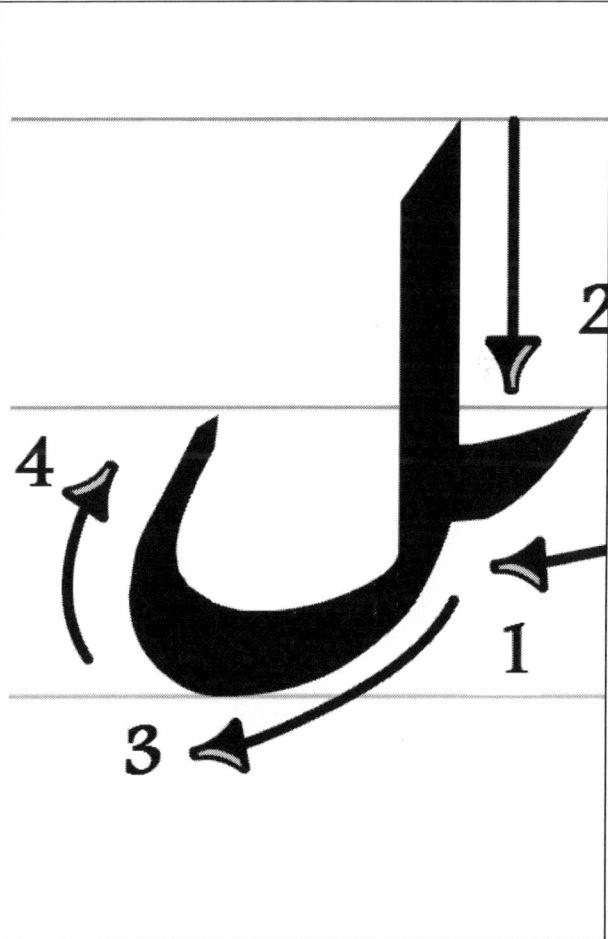

كبير

This shape of ك connects with all other letters. Any tooth in a word should lean to the right

To write the isolated haa hold your pen at 60 degrees and draw three dots (ruq'ah style). Then draw a column resembling alif but leaning slightly to the right, then draw a medial faa or qaaf. The letter looks like an oval leaning to the right.

This type of ك always connects these ascending letters:. ا لا ل ك

كلام
كارم

كلكتا

Calcutta. India

شباك

When making this curve circle back around to point at the beginning of the letter ك.

كسكس

س leans downward like any other horizontal line.

سكان

This shape looks like the كاف at the beginning of a word.
The ن in this style should be written at a downward angle.

مكتبة

There should always be an obtuse angle between the ك sign and the shape that looks like الف; these two together constitute the letter ك.

This separation occurs slightly above the line.

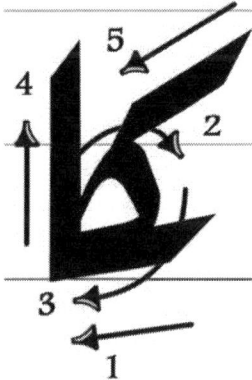

Remember that this style of لام does not dip below the line.

Remember that the connected alif is longer than the stand-alone alif. The curvatures of the letter لام look like the curvatures of the letters ن س ص ي.

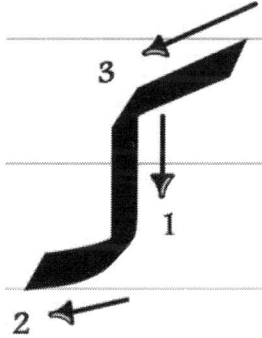

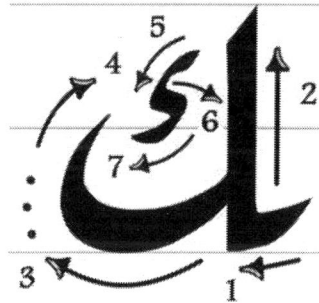

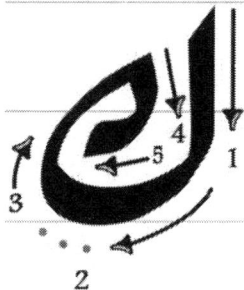

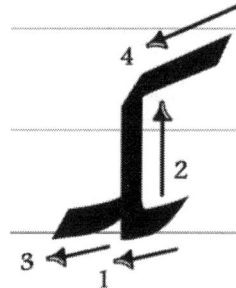

Drawing the Stand-alone miim

Hold your pen at 80 degrees. The head of the miim starts one and a half to two dots above the baseline. Stroke downward with the full width of the pen, and then continue with a gradual, diagonal line to the left. Then drop down past the baseline for three dots. The part connected to the head is drawn downward like any horizontal line. The stand-alone miim should look like a cat lying on a windowsill, looking out the window with its tail hanging down.

The head of the letter ميم is always filled in; the two sides below the head should be of equal length	This side should always lean downward. / In addition, this side should be leaning to the right.	The connection between the two sides should be curved and smooth, not sharp; also, the connecting angle should be around ninety–five degrees.	There should always be an obtuse angle between the head and the top area of the body.

مهدى مسلم معلم أحمد إيمان أميرة سميرة

معمل حمام محمد محمود الحمد المرأة

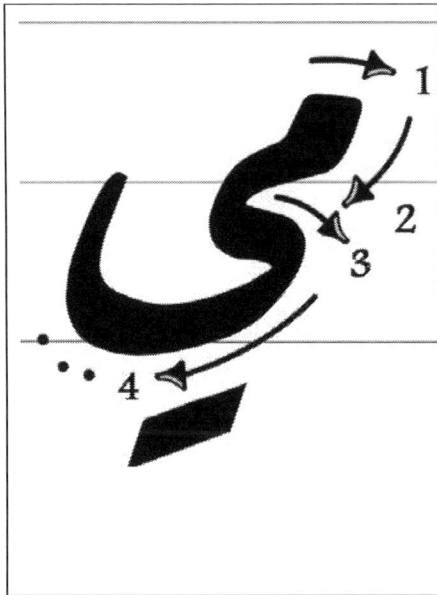

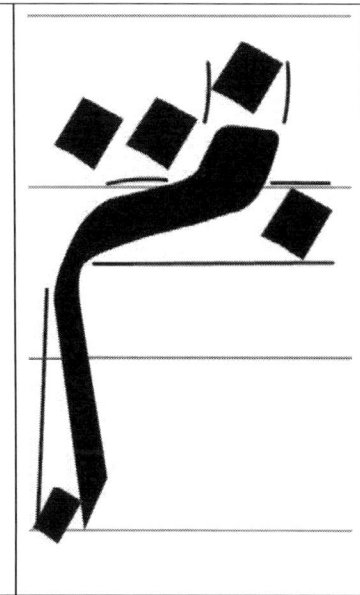

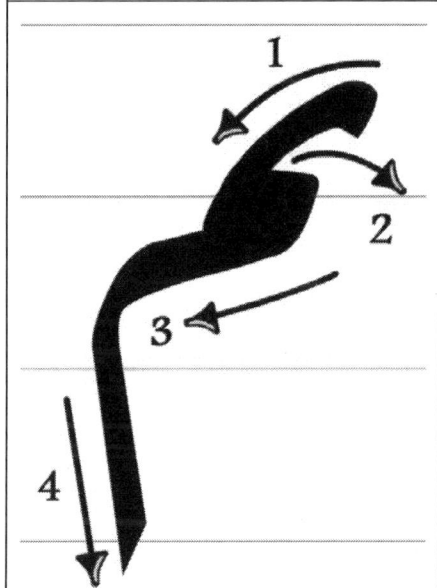

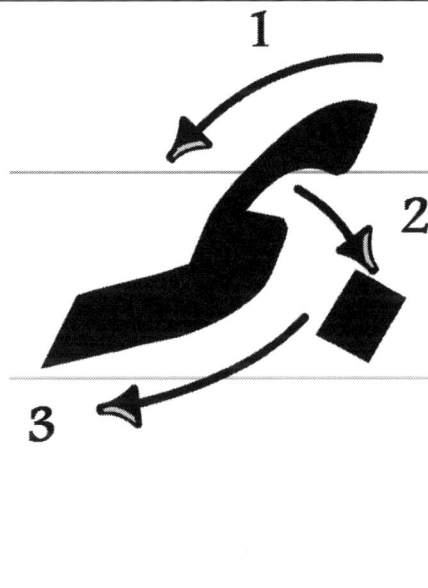

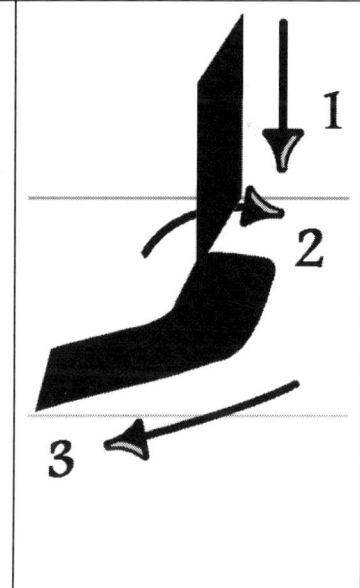

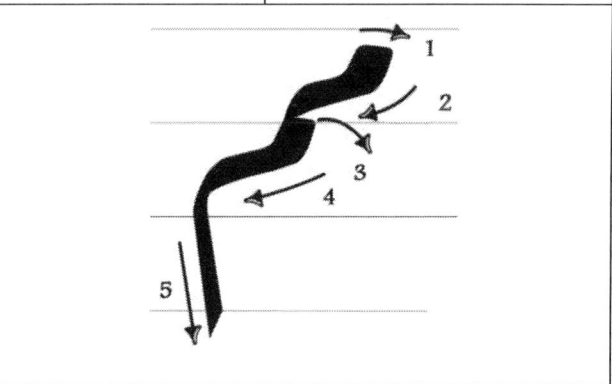

Drawing the Stand-alone nuun

Hold your pen at a 55 or 60-degree angle. Start two dots above the baseline. Make a stroke the length of one dot, and then curve out to the left as you approach the baseline, for the length of one and a half dots. Then curve up to one and a half dots above the baseline. Then either draw a dot in the middle of the letter or attach the dot to the end of the letter. There are two ways to do this. The first is one dot on the inside of the tail. The second one is attaching the three dots (joined together in ruq'ah style) to the outside of the tail.

The stand-alone نون has two shapes.

The first shape:

The first part looks exactly like the letter دال but with a slight curve. The dot occurs in the middle of the curved area. Notice that the letter does not dip below the line. The curved area touches the line then moves upward and maintains the curve. This rounded area looks like the rounded area found in the letters ل ي ص س.

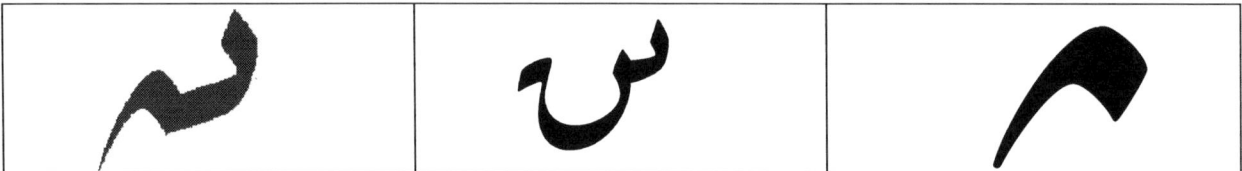

The second shape:

The first part of the second shape looks like the دال.

The beginning and end areas should be parallel. The end of the letter is similar to the three dots.

نون at the end of a word

Notice that the dot is a little bit higher, the area that connects the نون to the part before it should be wide and curved.

The beginning of the letter should be higher than the end.

This part of the letter should lean downward like all other vertical lines.

Remember that the end of ش and ض has the same shape as النون المتصلة, which means that the dots are attached to the body.

When نون comes at the beginning or the middle of a word, it should have a tooth like ي ث ت ب.

نب نت نـ ـنـ

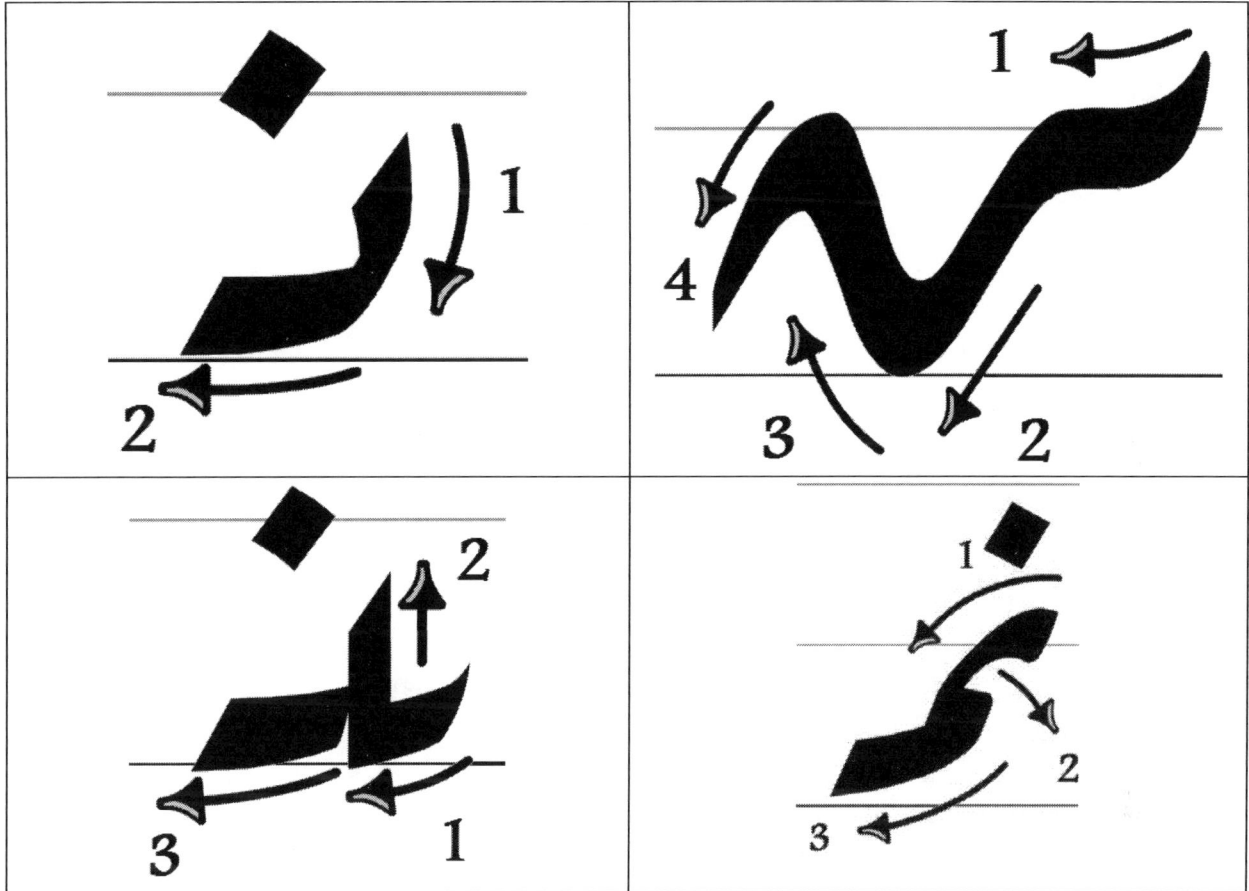

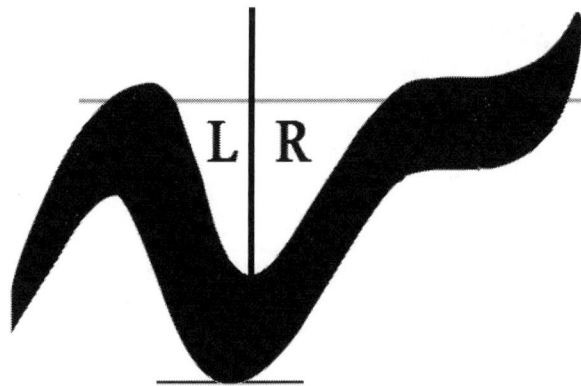

Notice that the right side is wider than the left side

فنان	أُسنان	إنسان
There are no purely horizontal lines in Ruq'ah script; all horizontal elements of a letter should be angled slightly downward.	The dot in the stand-alone نون should be on the same horizontal line as the beginning of the letter. You will start the rounded portion just after completing the very thin section.	The first part of the letter نون looks like first half of the letter الف but with a slight curve. The curvature of the نون is a continuous smooth rounded shape with no interruption.
بناء	نعناع	النور
	العين in the middle of a word is similar to م. The curvature of العين looks like the curvature found in ج, ح, and خ.	The rounded part of الواو is similar to the rounded part of ر and ز.
سه	حنين	بنين
The area referred to by the arrows is not teeth but sharp rounded edges.		The dot of النون is a bit higher than the beginning of the letter when the letter is connected.

When النون occurs in the beginning or the middle of a word it looks like الباء when it is in the beginning or middle of a word.

The letter هاء is comprised of three parts:

The first area looks like three big dots.

The second area looks like half of الف.

The last part looks like قاف or فاء with no dots.

If you combine these three parts, you will form the letter هاء.

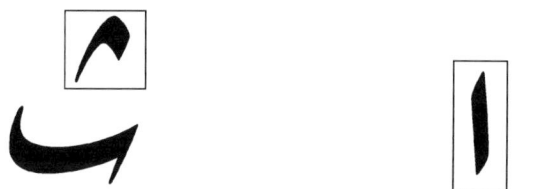

ش ف ـفـ ا

ه اثقـ

ا

شـ

ف قف

Notice that the loop of the letters فاء and قاف both lean to the right.

Remember that this part leans slightly to the left, do not draw it pointed straight up as you do when writing the الف.

Notice the space between the beginning and middle parts.

Also, notice that the initial curved area is not pointy though the curve is a sharp one.

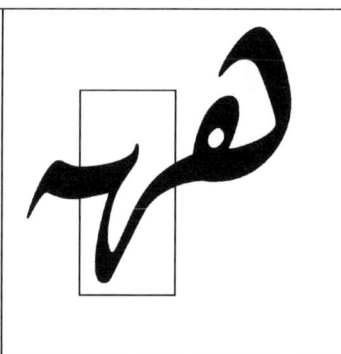

No sharp tooth in this area.

الهاء in the middle of a word:

91

طاء in the middle looks like the Arabic number seven.

The right side of the Arabic number seven is the only part of this shape that has a slight curve. The second side can be written either as a straight vertical line or as a vertical line that angles slightly to the right. The dash that connects the letter طاء to the following letter can be written as a short line either with slanted ends or as a short horizontal line that is angled slightly downward.

طاء at the end of a word:

Notice that it leans sharply to the left and is curved.

Isolated/stand-alone طاء should have an oval shape and lean to the right. The inner space should be less than the full thickness of the pen.

This is another shape of the letter طاء that resembles the number 7 in Arabic (or the letter V in English). This form is seen much more often in the everyday, "common usage" of ruq'ah script.

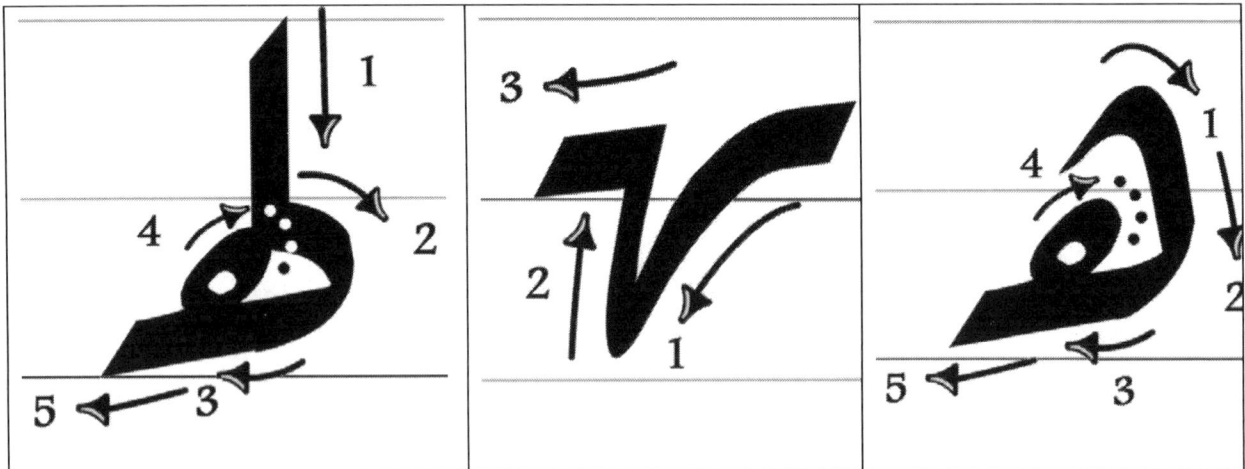

هم	له	هجة
قبعة / سجه	بر	و

The curved part of ياء is similar to the curved part of the letters ل ن ص س.	1- The initial stroke has a rather tight curve. 2- Drawn with the full width of the pen, leaning slightly downward to the right.	This middle curve protrudes slightly beyond the top part.

Different Shapes of the Final yaa:

The final yaa will take this shape when it is preceded by the tooth of the baa, taa, thaa, nuun, or yaa, the third tooth of the siin, or the tooth of the Saad.

حبى حتى حنى

ياء looks like any of these letters: ب ت ث ن, when found in the beginning or middle of a word.

يبيتيث

94

1 ﻰﻧ ﻰﺗ ﻰﻓ ﻰﻳ

2 ﻰﻣ ﻰﺣ

1. The final yaa will take this shape when it is preceded by the letters baa, taa, thaa, nuun, yaa, laam, kaaf, faa, qaaf.

2. 2. The final yaa will take this shape when it is preceded by jiim, Haa, khaa, ayn, ghayn, miim, haa, Taa, or DHaa.

The two areas of the letters ي and ح are identical.	Note that the first part of the letter ياء is removed.	Notice that there is no sharp point in this curved area.

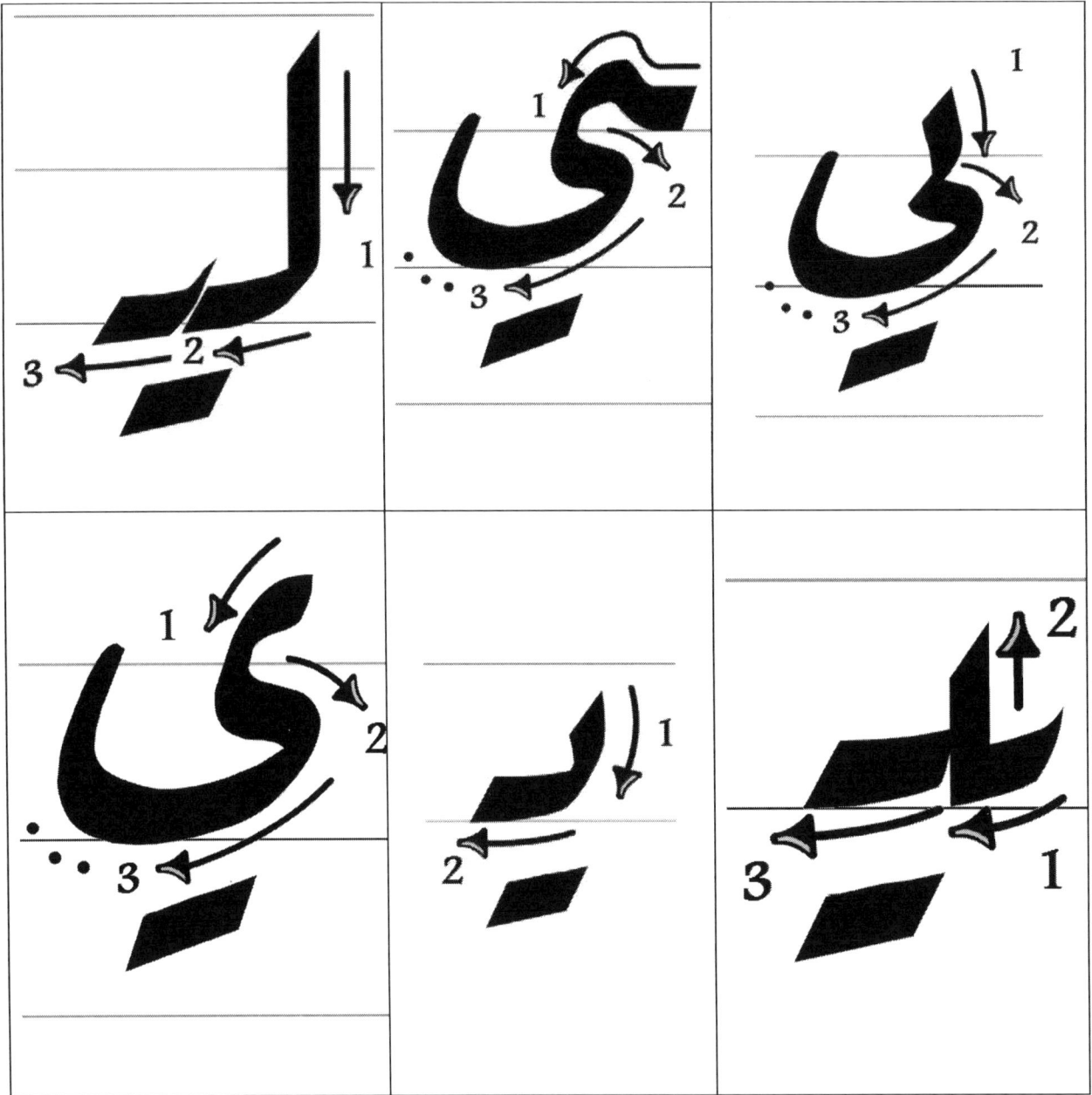

Made in the USA
Lexington, KY
29 August 2016